Do-It-Yourself
Marketing

Do-It-Yourself
Marketing

◈

DAVID F. RAMACITTI

American Management Association
New York · Atlanta · Boston · Chicago · Kansas City · San Francisco · Washington, D.C.
Brussels · Mexico City · Tokyo · Toronto

Library of Congress Number: 94-70816

Ramacitti, David F.

    Do-it-yourself marketing/David F. Ramacitti.
         p.   cm.
    Includes index.
    ISBN: 0-8144-7800-X

Printing number

10 9 8 7 6 5 4 3 2 1

For
Nancy—VSL!

Contents

Preface

Just before starting this book, I took a brief trip to our local shopping mall. As malls go, it is not particularly spectacular, especially compared to malls like Woodfield, near Chicago, or the supermall near Calgary, Canada. In fact, it has only 184 stores, so it's a fairly typical mall. I walked around the mall and just counted. I found:

- Fifteen places where you can buy men's ties
- Thirty-four stores in which you can get blue jeans
- Ten shops featuring women's shoes
- Fourteen retailers where you can find gifts
- Eight stores where you can buy greeting cards
- Twenty-three places where you can get something to eat
- Five jewelry shops
- Nine retailers offering paintings, posters, or art for your walls
- Twelve stores in which you can buy athletic shoes
- Five major department stores

This is just one of three malls in our area, to say nothing of the several dozen other shopping centers and retail districts scattered around the landscape.

Today's shopping mall, I believe, is a kind of microcosm of what the small-business marketer in virtually any field faces when he or she opens a business. The fact is that today's customer has many more products to choose from and many more suppliers to buy them from than he or she could ever possibly use.

Although the typical shopping mall focuses on selling to the general consumer, I would suggest that the situation is pretty much the same for all other small businesses as well: service businesses, professional offices, manufacturers, hospitality and tourism enterprises, health care providers, and financial services.

I would further suggest that it is equally true for nonprofit human service or health-related agencies and volunteer groups of all kinds. While for-profit businesses look for paying customers, nonprofits and volunteer groups seek contributors, members, or clients. Just ask any agency director how many "competitors" he or she has for government grants or the charitable dollar, or ask any service club membership chairperson how many "competitors" he or she has for new members or for attendees at charitable events.

It is a fundamental assumption of this book that your customers always have a choice. With perhaps a few very rare exceptions in esoteric high-tech fields, the fact is that your customers do not have to buy from you. They can find exactly the same product or service, or certainly a suitable substitute, from someone else—often at a cheaper price or in a more convenient location or in more colors or sizes or with free delivery or with better quality.

It is another fundamental assumption of this book that to survive, let alone prosper and grow, in today's hypercompetitive marketplace, you cannot sit back and wait for customers—or contributors or members—to materialize at your doorstep. You have to go out after them. Everything in this book flows out of this assumption. If you don't buy into it, there's no point in reading any further.

Finally, it is a fundamental assumption of this book that you have to promote, advertise, publicize—you have to market! Marketing is not a "wouldn't it be nice if we had the money" or a "we'll get around to it when we have the time" option, it is a survival imperative! The only question is how you will market, not whether. We explore exactly what marketing is more fully in Chapter 1.

While *Do-It-Yourself Marketing* can stand on its own, it is also a companion book to my two earlier books, *Do-It-Yourself Publicity* [New York: AMACOM, 1990] and *Do-It-Yourself Advertising* [New York: AMACOM, 1992]. As is obvious from their titles, those volumes explored two of the major components of marketing: paid media advertising and free editorial coverage (publicity).

Those who have read either or both of my other books will recognize some common threads or themes in this book, for two reasons:

1. These are important fundamental concepts that apply to one degree or another to all areas of promotion and marketing.
2. Since each book is designed to stand alone (i.e., you don't have to have read one in order to get something out of another), these important topics need to be repeated. But nothing is just copied verbatim; the discussion of each concept has been adapted to the special needs of this volume.

A good example is the concept of target or niche marketing: It is talked about a number of times in *Do-It-Yourself Publicity*, there is a whole chapter on it in *Do-It-Yourself Advertising*, and an entire chapter is devoted to it in this volume as well.

WHAT WE'LL BE COVERING

While publicity, the positive mention of a business or product in the news portions of the print or electronic media, and paid advertising, the buying of space or air time to advertise a business or product, may be the two most visible ways of promoting a business, they are by no means the only ways. *Do-It-Yourself Marketing* fills in the gaps, telling you

- How marketing is defined (I think you just might be surprised).
- What some of the dangerous myths that too many inexperienced marketers labor under are—for example, that all buyers base their purchase decisions on rational analysis.
- Why marketing is much more than just how you promote your business—advertising and marketing are not interchangeable.
- Which elements of your marketing program you can control (there are surprisingly few) and which ones you can't.
- Why not everyone in a given marketplace is or can be your potential customer.
- Why it is absolutely essential that you establish your own unique image in the minds of your customers and potential customers.

- Why for most businesses personal selling is by far the most important single element in the marketing program.
- Why how a business looks and feels to the customer, even including what the customer hears (do you play music over a storewide speaker system or when you put phone callers on hold?), is an important element in its marketing program.
- Why open houses, special events, and other activities can reach customers in important ways no other promotion can.
- Why you should probably be using more direct mail to promote your business (since, in my experience, it is a very underused promotional tool for small businesses).
- How to write a marketing plan for your small business, nonprofit, or volunteer group—it need not be a long and arduous task.

Finally, at the end of many of the chapters, you will find a section called "Getting Started Tomorrow Morning." Any organization can relatively easily develop grand plans for achieving some glorious goals. But these plans often falter because, while everyone agrees on the goal, no one is quite sure how to take the first step. "Getting Started Tomorrow Morning" is about first steps. It is designed to help you get your feet wet in the waters of marketing—remember how as kids we used to tell mom and dad that the pool or the lake wasn't bad once you got in?

WHO MY READERS ARE AND WHAT THEY NEED

Whether you're conscious of it or not—and, by the way, you should be—if you offer a product or service in a marketplace, you are making assumptions about who your customers are and what they need. This book is a product being offered in a marketplace, and I have, indeed, made a number of assumptions about who I think my future customers will be and what they need.

My target audience for this book is the literally millions of owners and/or hands-on managers of small businesses: retailers of every kind, service providers, professional offices, restaurants, bed and breakfasts, motels, jobbers of all sorts, and manufacturers of plastic, metal, or wood products.

My target audience for this book is also the directors of the hundreds of thousands of small nonprofit agencies in this country, from colleges or private schools to health or human service agencies.

And my target audience for this book is the members of the innumerable volunteer organizations—church and youth groups, booster clubs, professional associations, service clubs, support groups of all kinds—who have somehow inherited the job of "marketing" their group and don't know where to start.

Among my assumptions about my readers are:

• You are indeed an owner or manager of a small business or agency. Your business is a lot more likely to have five or ten employees than it is to have 50 or 100, to say nothing of 500 or 1,000.

• You are going to be marketing your business or organization to a fairly well-defined local or, at most, regional market area. The only exception to this might be a small specialty manufacturer who is distributing products on a national basis, but to a fairly well-defined market group.

• This means, in turn, that you are going to be dealing almost entirely with local media and/or putting together local promotional efforts. You might be working with trade publications that circulate nationally, but again to fairly closely defined target groups. And you certainly will not be contemplating placing ads on national TV networks or in nationally circulated general consumer magazines or newspapers.

• You are a hands-on owner or manager when it comes to marketing. You do not have a marketing manager on staff, nor do you have an advertising or public relations agency on retainer.

• You have little or no previous background or training in the specifics of marketing.

• You have very limited time.

• And, finally, you have very limited resources, especially money.

GOALS OF THIS BOOK

The goals of *Do-It-Yourself Marketing* are to:

- Familiarize you with the basic concepts of marketing.
- Help you apply these concepts to your individual business or organization and adapt them to the unique aspects of your particular market situation.
- Help you develop specific marketing goals for your business, nonprofit organization, or group.
- Suggest specific marketing techniques or programs suitable for your business or organization.
- Help you start writing a basic marketing plan for your business, nonprofit group, or club.

This is a book about basics. If we have to choose between being too simplistic and getting bogged down in complexity, we'll definitely lean toward the former. We will always choose the practical approach—what will work in the real world of tight budgets and overworked small-business owners or managers.

I have always thought of marketing as the ultimate chess game—only in marketing, instead of having just one opponent, you have to meet the challenge of multiple competitors. And in marketing, the marketplace itself (perhaps analogous to the chessboard?) changes, presenting you with yet more challenges. Good luck!

Do-It-Yourself
Marketing

1

What Is Marketing?

ANECDOTE 1: I'm writing this book on my seven-year-old Compaq Deskpro computer with word processing software. It is my first computer.

When I set out to buy it, I would go into a computer retailer, hand the first salesperson I saw my business card, and say, "I'm looking for a small-business computer."

Here is what I thought I was doing:

- I was giving that salesperson my name, address, and phone number so that he or she would have the opportunity to follow up.
- By saying I wanted a "small-business" computer, I was indicating that I was willing to spend more than the few hundred dollars that their "el cheapo" model would cost. In other words, I was a customer with some money.

At one place, the salespeople seemed to be engaged in an extremely absorbing conversation and failed to notice my interest in their products. So I left.

At another place, the salesperson to whom I handed my card looked perplexed, glanced around hurriedly, and said, "Oh, well, uh, George does small-business computers, but he just went to lunch. He'll be back in an hour or so." I left.

In yet another place, the salesperson smiled, waved her arms toward a long wall where a half dozen computers were lined up, their screens glowing brightly, and said, "These are our newest models. Wanna try one?" Again, I left.

ANECDOTE 2: For my business clothing, I prefer a traditional or classic look, rather than trendy fads. So when I'm in the market for a new tie or a new sport coat and I walk into a men's clothing store, if I hear rock music blaring over the speaker system, I turn around and leave.

ANECDOTE 3: I have a local supermarket where, if you stop one of the store personnel in the aisle and ask something like "Where can I find birthday candles?" that person will smile, instantly drop whatever it is he or she is doing, and take you right to the spot, even if it's on the other side of the store. I do virtually all of my food shopping there.

ANECDOTE 4: There is a local restaurant that has great "izza." But it also has great potholes in its gravel parking lot, the outside of the restaurant hasn't been painted in years, and the *P* in its neon sign has been out for as long as I can remember. I rarely go there to eat.

All of these folks are "marketing"—and probably don't even realize it.

DEFINITIONS OF MARKETING

The American Marketing Association says: "Marketing is the process of planning and executing the conception, pricing, promotion and distribution of ideas, goods and services to create exchanges that satisfy individual and organizational objectives." [*Marketing News*, March 1, 1985, Vol. 19, No. 5, p. 1.]

According to Northwestern University's Philip Kotler, who is generally acknowledged to be "the" expert on modern marketing, "Marketing is a social process by which individuals and groups obtain what they need and want through creating and exchanging products and value with others." [*Marketing Management: Analysis, Planning and Control*, Englewood Cliffs, N.J.: Prentice-Hall, 1984.]

But my favorite definition of marketing comes from business guru Peter Drucker: "Marketing is so basic that it cannot be considered a separate function. . . . It is the whole business seen from the point of view of its final result, that is, from the customer's point of view." [*Practice of Management*, New York: HarperCollins, 1953.]

Drucker's definition is my favorite for two reasons. First, because he aptly points out that no matter what specific business we might think we're in, in the end we're a marketing organization. Sooner or later we somehow have to deal with customers. This applies whether we're "selling" goods and services to consumers in the general marketplace or "selling" the services of a nonprofit organization to funding sources or to clients.

Second, and I think more important, because Drucker puts the emphasis in marketing where it belongs: on the customer! I'll have more to say about this in a moment.

I can hear you thinking, "Come on, that's too simple. It's gotta be more complicated than that. What's the catch?"

The catch is that often a seemingly very simple and straightforward concept can be very difficult and complex in its real-world implementation. In and of itself, marketing is a very simple concept.

Once upon a time, if I was good at making flint arrowheads and you were good at making clay pots, we exchanged, so that both of us had what we needed. I produced only as many arrowheads as the hunters in our tribe used, and you produced only as many clay pots as our village needed. The marketplace was uncomplicated and easily balanced, and each of us had a well-defined and clearly understood place in it, both as producer and as consumer.

Today there are a dozen different arrowhead makers producing arrowheads in various grades of quality and for various kinds of specialized functions, and there are a dozen different clay pot makers producing pots in different sizes and shapes and adorning them in various ways. And in total, the producers are turning out far more arrowheads and far more clay pots than the marketplace can possibly absorb. This means that as consumers we can pick and choose, according to our needs and wants, from an assortment of products that is much larger than we need or can use, and that as producers we have to compete for the attention of the consumer.

MARKETING DOES NOT EQUAL ADVERTISING

Even if I accomplish nothing else with this book, I want to get you to understand that marketing is a broad concept that encompasses virtually everything you do that touches on your customers, however you define them. One of the most common and most serious mistakes the inexperienced marketer makes is to assign a too-narrow definition to marketing.

Marketing is not synonymous with advertising. Advertising is just one function of marketing.

Your sales reps are engaged in a marketing activity. So are the person who answers your phone and the person who mows your grass, waters your plants, and sweeps up.

Your organization's logo and the sign on the front of your building are marketing tools. So is the music you play over your phone system while you have someone on hold.

News releases you send to the local media about a new product you are introducing or about your twenty-fifth anniversary in business are part of your marketing effort. So is a talk you are asked to give to the Optimists Club.

Do your employees wear uniforms? Are you open nights or Saturdays? Do you deliver? Do you offer free gift wrapping?

Do you ever have an open house for your customers or send them a newsletter? Are you a stickler for following policy, or do you encourage your people to bend the rules if they have to in order to solve a customer's problem?

These are all marketing activities.

The perceptive reader will have noticed that these are all various forms of promotion—personal sales, paid advertising, publicity, special events, public relations, direct mail, store decor, and customer service.

There are only four major categories of marketing activities: promotion, price, place, and product (or service)—the famous Four Ps. We will explore the Four Ps a bit more fully in Chapter 3. Suffice it to say at this point that in this book I will focus mainly on the promotional aspects of marketing.

THE MARKETING UMBRELLA

I like to think of marketing as a huge umbrella. The braces or struts that give the umbrella its basic shape and hold it together are like the major components of marketing: product (what you offer to the marketplace), price (what you charge for it), place (where you decide to offer it), and promotion (how you let people know about it). Covering the struts and, at the same time, connecting them is the fabric of the umbrella. It is what makes the umbrella useful.

In our marketing umbrella, the fabric is all of the many specific and concrete ways you choose to relate to your customers. And all these myriad marketing decisions, big and small, are interconnected and interrelated. If you'll allow me to stretch my umbrella analogy, just as with the umbrella, if you push too hard on one side, this will affect the shape on the other side.

CUSTOMER FOCUS

Never lose your focus on the customer. I cannot stress strongly enough, or often enough, Drucker's observation that marketing is the *whole* business (emphasis mine) as seen from the customer's point of view. It is an undercurrent that you will see again and again throughout this book.

Saying that your marketing efforts should be focused on the customer ought to be as obvious as announcing that the sun came up today. However, like the sun coming up, we tend to take customers for granted and therefore mostly pay lip service to being customer-driven.

It's so easy for us to get caught up in the myriad details of the day-to-day operation of our business. As a result, what I call "organizational conveniences," as opposed to "customer conveniences," can creep into the picture and, after a while, dominate our business without us even noticing it.

Examples of organizational conveniences are

- Playing rock music over the store's loudspeakers because that's what the sales clerks like to listen to, even though the customers may not
- Not being open evenings or weekends
- Not having enough incoming phone lines, so that customers calling in usually get a busy signal
- Sending out sale announcements by bulk rate postage, even though the announcement sometimes doesn't get to the customer until after the sale is over

- Not having enough sales clerks or using inexperienced and poorly trained people because it's cheaper

Everything your business does (everything!) sooner or later affects the customer. Therefore, virtually every business decision you make needs to be considered in a "marketing" context: "Will this decision enhance or detract my relationship with my customers?"

MARKETING ANECDOTES, REVISITED

ANECDOTE 1, buying my computer. As far as I was concerned, all of the so-called salespeople mentioned in my little anecdote (which, by the way, is a true story) were more interested in satisfying their own needs—the need to carry on their own conversations, the need not to have to learn all about their products, the need not to be bothered—than they were in meeting my needs.

I eventually bought my computer at the shop where, when I walked in, the salesperson handed me a cup of coffee, took me to a little conference room, sat down with a clipboard, and said, "Okay, how are you going to use this computer? Have you worked on a computer before? What kinds of information will you be putting into it? What kinds of information do you want out of it?" And so on. In other words, the salesperson was concerned about my needs first.

By the way, I have no idea whether I paid more, about the same, or less for my computer at the place where I bought it than I would have elsewhere. I do know that every time I've called with a question about the software, the staff has patiently answered my question, walking me through the answer. And I know where I'm going to buy my next computer. In fact, I've got my eye on this great little laptop. . . .

ANECDOTE 2, buying traditional business clothing. I don't shop in places with rock music blaring over the speaker system for two reasons.

First, I don't like rock.

Second, I assume that the store's products are geared toward "kids" (the under-twenty-five set), of which I definitely am not one. In fact, that clothing store may very well have an excellent selection of classic men's suits and sport coats somewhere in the back of the store, but I never get past the entrance because as far as I'm concerned, the rock music is advertising that the store doesn't have what I want.

ANECDOTE 3, the friendly supermarket. Like everyone else these days, I'm busy. Shopping, especially for everyday items like food, is not an entertainment for me, it's a chore. So the last thing I want to do is hunt up one aisle and down another for what I need.

I'm impressed by the people in the supermarket where I shop for two reasons. First, they all know their merchandise. There's no fumbling around trying to find the person who takes care of this section or that. Second, if they are willing to drop what they're doing without a moment's hesitation, that says to me that they genuinely think that customer convenience is more important than organizational convenience.

ANECDOTE 4, the "izza" restaurant. Since the restaurant does not place any kind of priority on keeping up its exterior appearance (potholes in the parking lot, the outside not painted, a sign that's never been fixed), I can't help but wonder if it is equally lackadaisical about cleanliness in its kitchen. Besides, there are lots of other places where I can get pizza that's nearly as good and where I don't have to worry about ruining the springs of my car. And there are lots more places where I can enjoy a meal out that isn't pizza.

I'm perfectly willing to admit that my attitudes may be both unreasonable and unfair. But I would also strongly suggest to you that lots and lots of consumers make decisions about what they buy and where they buy it based on equally unreasonable and unfair attitudes.

In clinical psychology and social work, there is an axiom that says, "You start where the patient is, not where you want him to be." In a sense the same can be said about marketing.

THE MYSTERY OF MARKETING

Finally, marketing is the myriad little details of your business and how they affect your customers. The rest of this book will focus on how you can be more aware of and exercise some measure of control over those details so as to maximize your opportunity to be successful in the marketplace.

But there is a very real and ever-present element in marketing that has to be touched on here, at least briefly, so that when you come across it, you don't scratch your head and wonder what happened or, worse, get so discouraged that you give up. It's what I call the mystery of marketing. The fact is that despite all our detailed analysis of the marketplace, despite all our exhaustive planning on how we will respond to the marketplace, and despite all our careful implementation of our marketing plans and programs, in any successful marketing effort there is always an element of the unknown at work.

No computer is large enough to know everything there is to know about the complex interplay of all the factors that are at work in even a small, local market. No plan can ever be detailed enough to anticipate every occurrence and have a prescribed response. (The federal government and big corporations try this with their thick, multivolume standard procedure manuals, but guess what? They still get taken by surprise all the time.) And no execution of a marketing program is ever flawless.

Instead of being discouraged by the fact that you can't control everything, you should be excited. If someone actually could get a big enough computer or develop a detailed enough marketing plan or execute a program perfectly enough, then, sooner or later, someone would. And then that person would own the marketplace, lock, stock, and barrel. There would be no opportunity for new competitors to try their ideas in the marketplace and maybe grab a share of the pie. The mystery of marketing is what makes marketing fun.

Getting Started Tomorrow Morning

Take a look at your own attitudes about where you shop and why. Get out a legal pad and draw a line down the middle, dividing it in half vertically. At the top of the left-hand column, write the word DO, and at the top of the right-hand column, write DON'T. Below is a list of shopping categories. For each category, here's what you should do:

- In the DO column, write the name of the specific place you most often go to when you want something in that category. Below that, list not more than two reasons why you go to that specific place. Keep your answers to ten or twelve words.

- In the DON'T column, write the name of a place you never go to when you want something in that category, even though you know the place probably has it. Below that, list one or two reasons why you don't go there. Again, keep your answers to ten or twelve words.

Be honest with your answers. Don't you buy some things from a place that's probably more expensive than others? Isn't there some place you actually go out of your way to do business with?

The idea of this exercise is to start to sensitize you to two things:

1. That everything you do that touches your customers is part of your marketing program
2. That to one degree or another we all make buying decisions based on factors that have little if anything to do with the inherent value of the product or the place we're buying it

Shopping Categories

- Casual clothing
- Fancy clothing
- Eating out
- Milk
- Other food
- Hardware items
- Movie rental
- Gasoline for the car
- Life or auto insurance
- Towels, sheets, and other linens

2

Ten Modern
Marketing Myths

If, indeed, all businesses are essentially marketing organiza-tions, then it's important for us to be aware of and to under-stand our beliefs about our customers, our marketplace, and our products. Or, to use the slang, to know "where we are coming from." These beliefs often take the form of basic assump-tions: We assume that x or y is true about our customer group, and we therefore make decisions based on that assumption. These can range from small, everyday things to decisions that may be crucial for our survival. For example:

- How and where we spend our promotion dollars
- Where we locate our business
- Which products or brands we offer
- How we price our products or services

Unfortunately, the business owner or manager who has little or no background in marketing is often only vaguely aware of these assumptions.

At best, he or she might have inherited some traditional beliefs about the industry, which may or may not be valid any longer. For example, the assumption that the only potential customers for mo-torcycles are scruffy, Hell's Angels types or teenagers looking for inexpensive transportation may be a serious marketing mistake. Haven't you noticed the convoys of middle-aged retired couples rid-ing their fully equipped Honda Goldwings (which, by the way, cost about as much as the average car) down the interstate?

At worst, the inexperienced marketer may create a lot of false assumptions based on his or her own biases, such as:

- I love country-western music, so all of my customers must like country-western music. Therefore, I'll spend most of my advertising dollars on the country-western radio station.
- Most old people live on fixed incomes and are therefore poor, so I won't target them as potential customers.
- Big businesses buy only from other big businesses, so I won't even make a call on that major manufacturer.

ASSUMPTIONS BECOME MYTHS

In fact, many of these assumptions get repeated over and over again, and are passed on from one business to another, from one generation to another, until they take on the status of myths. A myth is defined as (1) a traditional story used to explain a phenomenon or custom; (2) any fictitious story, person, or thing.

The problem with myths is that there is often some small element of truth in them—a lot of motorcycle riders are Hell's Angels types; a lot of old people do live on fixed incomes; a lot of big businesses do buy most of their supplies from other big businesses. Myths can be very powerful. They tend to take on a life of their own. We start to accept them as absolute truisms, rarely questioning their validity or relevance to a changed world.

My experience with hundreds of small start-up businesses, especially those whose owners or managers have little or no marketing experience, is that those owners and managers do, indeed, tend to buy into certain myths about marketing. Unfortunately, they often make some ill-advised decisions based on those myths. They waste a lot of time and money and go through a lot of frustration and exasperation. Sometimes they actually endanger their businesses without ever realizing that their actions are based on a myth that is no longer valid, if it ever was.

Over the years I've collected what I consider to be the ten most common modern marketing myths.

Myth 1: The Rational Buyer

As owners or managers of businesses or nonprofit organizations, we're trained to approach all our decisions rationally. We're supposed to gather all the relevant facts, analyze them, look at the options, weigh the trade-offs, including cost, and then decide on the best course. This process gets to be so much a part of our routine that we take it for granted; we're hardly even conscious that we're doing it.

The great danger here is that because this has become so much of a habit for us, as business owners or managers, we assume that everyone else makes their buying decisions on the same rational basis. We start to believe that all of our customers look at the pluses and minuses, weigh the price choices, consider the trade-offs, and then make rational buying decisions.

So we tend to base all of our customer approaches and promotions on this assumption. For instance, our sales brochures and ads tend to stress the features of the product, often slipping into technical explanations and even industry jargon to try to make their point.

The truth is that while some consumer buying decisions are indeed based on rational thought processes, most purchases are influenced much more by factors like emotions and feelings, personal prejudices, peer pressure, brand loyalty, and just plain convenience.

This is particularly true of:

- Impulse products, things we tend to buy on the spur of the moment, like a meal at a fast food restaurant or a donut and a cup of coffee or a can of Pepsi
- Consumer products, such as television sets, clothing, and records or CDs
- Frequently purchased items, like breakfast cereals or household cleaners
- Lower-priced items, such as chewing gum or candy bars

In other words, most of the things we buy!

Myth 2: The Magic Answer

I consider this to be one of the most insidious and dangerous of the marketing myths. Why? Because it is so pervasive, because it can take so many devious forms, and because it simply will not die.

The essence of the myth is that in any given situation there is a

Magic Answer that will solve all our problems, if we can just find it. We go to workshops and seminars in search of the Magic Answer. We read books and magazines in search of the Magic Answer. We talk to other businesspeople, our friends, our spouse, even our brother-in-law (whom we dislike and think is an idiot!) in search of the Magic Answer.

One of the most common forms of the Magic Answer Myth is the Magic Medium Myth. It assumes that there is one advertising medium that will work for everybody in all situations. This, of course, is often television, since it is the most glamorous and certainly the most visible of the media. The rationale goes something like this: "If we could just afford to be on TV, we'd have more customers than we could handle!" However, for many small, narrowly focused businesses, TV may be the worst choice as an advertising medium!

Another form that's particularly dear to my heart is the Magic Consultant Myth, because I've found myself trapped on the wrong end of that expectation. The Magic Consultant Myth holds that if you just bring in an "outside expert," he or she will provide all the answers and your business will become an instant success.

Of course, there is no Magic Answer, no Magic Medium, no Magic Consultant. There never has been, and there never will be. At first glance that may seem rather discouraging. But, if you think about it for a moment, that might not be all bad. If there were a Magic Answer, someone would probably have discovered it by now in virtually every industry. It would logically follow that whoever found that Magic Answer would probably totally dominate that industry. This, in turn, would mean that there would be no opportunity for an entrepreneur to start a new business in that industry. The very fact that there are no Magic Answers is what gives a new business at least a fighting chance to carve out a piece of the market for itself.

Myth 3: The Knockout Punch

The Knockout Punch myth, and its variations, like the Big Breakthrough myth, is a kind of corollary to the Magic Answer myth. It normally goes something like this: "If we could just find the right opportunity (Magic Answer), we could really take a big chunk of market share away from the competition (deliver a Knockout Punch)."

The problem is that the lore of entrepreneuring is rife with these stories. They are the staples of the books and magazines that would-be business owners devour. The folks who were smart (lucky?) enough to buy a McDonald's franchise in the late 1950s or get into the video rental business in the early 1980s. The "nobody" who had an idea, pursued it with persistence, and, to one degree or another, was fortunate enough to be in the right place at the right time, and hit it big.

There's no question that these things do happen. Businesses, either through brilliant imagination or just dumb luck, often introduce a new product or service, or develop a major variation on an existing product or service, and take their competition completely by surprise.

Unfortunately, this is very much the exception rather than the rule. There are lots of clarinet players, but there are very few Benny Goodmans.

Most fights are won on points, not knockouts. Most races are won by inches, not lengths. Most businesses succeed through lots of small day-to-day victories, not a breakthrough that puts their competition out of business.

This is one of the many paradoxes one finds in marketing.

On the one hand, every business owner or manager is always on the lookout for the breakthrough opportunity, to some extent chasing a rainbow:

- The market niche that hasn't been filled—for example, Chrysler's introduction of the mini-van, which practically ran the traditional station wagon off the road
- The new promotional medium that really reaches the desired audience—for instance, cable's MTV, which quickly became "the" way to reach teenagers
- The new product that literally takes a market segment by storm, as Teenage Mutant Ninja Turtles did among youngsters

Unfortunately, such breakthrough opportunities are rare. I am certainly never going to tell entrepreneurs not to chase dreams, because that's what entrepreneurs are: dreamers. But what most businesses have to understand is that they are not going to succeed by knocking out their competition. Rather, they are going to succeed by carving out a small but significant market share in gradual increments.

Myth 4: We Have No Competition

A few years ago one of the Big Three automakers actually ran a TV ad in which it used the words "we have no competition." I remember being mildly insulted by the ad, thinking to myself, "How dumb do they think I am?" As if I'd never heard of the other two members of the Big Three, let alone Honda, Toyota, Nissan, Mercedes-Benz, and so on.

Today, at just one auto dealer in our medium-size urban market—a so-called megadealer—you can choose from twelve different brands of cars.

Along one busy street in the town where I live, there are a McDonald's, a Hardee's, a Pizza Hut, a Godfather's Pizza, a Taco Bell, a Long John Silver's, a Red Lobster, a Bishop's Buffet, and two other nonfranchise eateries (a Chinese restaurant and a family restaurant) all within a mile of one another.

Whether we're talking about the worldwide marketplace that automakers and fast food franchises compete in or just the local marketplace in which a small retail shop might compete, the fact is that all of today's marketplaces are overproducted, overretailed, and overpromoted! Everyone has competition. Period.

It might take the form of head-to-head competition, such as burger joints like McDonald's and Wendy's across the street from each other. Or it might be indirect, like a Pizza Hut and a Taco Bell near each other. But make no mistake about it, no matter what business you're in, you have competition. To assume you don't is to put yourself in a fool's paradise.

Myth 5: The Better Mousetrap

This is another one of my favorites. It holds that if I just invent the better mousetrap, then everyone will beat a path to my door. It has lots of permutations, like "Our products are so good, they sell them-selves" and "Our reputation is our best advertising."

Unfortunately, more often than not this is simply an excuse to justify not spending any money on marketing, advertising, or pro-motion.

The fact is, today's marketplace is filled to overflowing with mousetraps, from generic versions to models loaded down with all sorts of high-tech bells and whistles. They come in all sizes and colors, made out of every imaginable kind of material; they're avail-able in practically any store you might enter and at virtually any price you want to pay. In other words, even if you could come up with a better mousetrap (which is unlikely in the first place), the chances are the marketplace would greet your astonishing inven-tion not with a thunderous stampede to your door, but with a disin-terested yawn!

Myth 6: Everyone Is Our Customer

In my experience, this is among the three or four most common myths bought into by the new and/or inexperienced marketer. Its basic tenet is that every living person in a given market area is a potential customer for a product or service.

This is an optimistic but very dangerous trap to fall into. Here are just a couple of illustrations of how buying into the myth can lead the marketer astray:

Believing that everyone in a given area (a certain part of town, a whole community, or maybe even a county or two) is a possible customer can all too easily lead would-be business owners to plug into their start-up business plan a market potential far larger than the actual potential. This, of course, results in completely unrealistic revenue forecasts. The would-be business owner may borrow money and make investments in buildings and/or equipment based on these unrealistic numbers. Then, when the projections aren't realized, the owner may get panicky and start making ill-advised decisions in a desperate attempt to make the numbers.

Once the business is open, believing that everyone in a given area is a potential customer might well steer the business owner toward an advertising program that reaches the largest number of people, which in most markets usually involves relatively high cost media like television, radio, and newspapers. In fact, if the business owner understood that the bulk of the potential customers were from a relatively small and rather specific segment of the market, he or she might choose a much more cost-efficient advertising program using media that deliver just that market segment.

The demographics of your market area (age, gender, income, occupation, family status), the products you offer (generic or name brands), how you price your products (low, moderate, or high end), your location (a low-rent part of town or a status address), your location relative to where your customers live or work and how they come and go, and last, but certainly not least, the relative strength of your competition in your market area are all factors whose interaction will tend to limit who your potential customers are going to be.

Myth 7: Price Is Everything

This is another candidate for top honors among common marketing myths. It holds that the only reason most people buy any given product is price—they will go where it's cheapest. Therefore, the only way to compete is to cut price.

The usual way this myth manifests itself is that whenever the owner of a small business is thinking about putting together some kind of promotion, the first thing he or she wants to do is to have a sale or run a coupon—in other words, cut price in one form or another.

There's no doubt that pricing is important. In fact, it is one of the most crucial marketing decisions you can make. The huge success of Wal-Mart, Kmart, and other price-oriented mass merchandisers is certainly ample proof that consumers love a bargain, or what they think is a bargain. However, I must remind you that this book was written not for the Wal-Marts of the world, but for small, more or less locally owned and operated businesses. For them to try to compete on price with the big boys, like Wal-Mart, is a real fool's game. They simply do not have the buying and/or staying power to play that game with the high-volume price cutters.

I'm reminded of the Saturday matinee Westerns I grew up with. Whenever the good guy was about to face the bad guy in a shootout, there was always the Big Question among the townspeople: "Which one is faster on the draw?" One of the townspeople, usually the wizened old barfly, would tell his fellow onlookers something like, "No matter how fast you think you are, there's always somebody a little faster."

Well, no matter how far down you think you can drive the price, there is always somebody who's willing to make it a little more cheaply and/or willing to accept a little less markup, and who therefore will undercut you in price.

Although price is a critical competitive factor, it is certainly not the only factor, especially for the small business.

Myth 8: We Don't Have to Promote

Whereas in the discussion of the Better Mousetrap Myth I was thinking mostly about new businesses, here I'm thinking more of the owners of successful, well-established businesses that fall into the trap of becoming complacent, even cocky. They start to believe that they "own" their customers, that they don't have to go out after new customers anymore, that the competition can't touch them.

This is yet another fool's paradise. In today's supercompetitive marketplace, if you're not talking to your customers or clients, reminding them why they trade with you and what you offer that the competition doesn't, you can be sure that someone else is telling them what it offers that you don't!

I am not underrating the importance of customer loyalty and positive word-of-mouth recommendations to a business. These are, and always will be, two of the most powerful competitive advantages any business can enjoy. Rather, what I am suggesting is that in today's supercompetitive marketplace, these may no longer be enough all by themselves to assure a business's continued success.

Myth 9: Just Make More Sales Calls (or Just Run More Ads)

This is sort of the opposite side of the same coin. Whereas some businesspeople get complacent and start thinking that their businesses are so good that they don't have to advertise or promote any more, others fall into the trap of thinking that promotion and/or advertising is the one and only Magic Answer.

They tell the sales department, "Just get out there and make more calls. It's a numbers game. The more calls you make, the more sales you'll make." They may be conveniently ignoring the fact that they haven't updated their product line in a decade, while their competition has.

They try cable TV or shoppers or magazines—in other words, whatever advertising medium they haven't already tried—with the expectation that if they just run enough ads, things will turn around. They may be paying no notice to the fact that the competitor down the street has just expanded and remodeled its store, and perhaps is now open more hours or has added free delivery and free gift wrapping.

Myth 10: How Can We Do It on the Cheap?

I debated with myself on whether to place this one first or last. There are times that I think it is the number one myth among small-business owners. They so rarely ask, "How can I do things well or right?" Instead, they ask, "What's the cheapest way?" I decided to put it last because people tend to remember most the last thing they've seen or heard.

Of course I understand that small-business owners and managers don't have deep pockets. If you'll recall, that's one of the fundamental assumptions I made about my readers. But I make a significant distinction between spending limited resources wisely and judiciously and always looking to do things on the cheap. Doing things on the cheap can lead to ill-advised marketing decisions like:

- Choosing an out-of-the-way (i.e., low-rent) location for your business when it is the kind of business that depends greatly on convenience and walk-in traffic
- Picking the cheapest advertising medium in your market, even though its audience really doesn't include a lot of your customers or potential customers
- Hiring only inexperienced, minimum-wage people when the high-tech nature of your products demands a knowledgeable sales staff

Getting Started Tomorrow Morning

Now come on, be honest with yourself. How many of these myths, or their variations, have you bought into in one form or another? Didn't you find yourself nodding your head in agreement once in a while? Maybe you even thought, "Oh boy, do I know that feeling!"

I still have a fascination with the Magic Answer myth. Even though intellectually I understand that an answer that works in one situation will work only in that situation and is not transferable, there is still a part of me that would like to believe that if I just read enough books and go to enough workshops and acquire enough experience, I can find the Magic Answer.

Don't be embarrassed. It's only human nature to want nice, neat explanations for what we see around us. That's why myths get started in the first place.

3

The Four Ps

ANECDOTE 1: A clothing retailer (of mostly jeans and sportswear) that I know uses a sophisticated inventory tracking and pricing system that starts an item at full price when it goes on display in his store, then automatically cuts the price by 10 percent every four or six weeks until it moves out. The key component in his marketing strategy is price.

ANECDOTE 2: Another friend of mine designed a new garden tool, a multipurpose hoe that had several cutting edges and could be used not only for general hoeing but for weeding, chopping, and even light pruning. He worked on the tool for many months, changing the length and shape of the cutting edges, varying the thickness of the blade, and adding a cutout so that dirt would pass through. He wrestled with questions like what kind of steel he should use in the blade: high carbon, which holds an edge better, or stainless, which won't corrode. For him, the key element in his marketing strategy was the product.

ANECDOTE 3: There's a local car dealer I know who came to this area about a decade ago. He bought one of the weaker auto dealerships (it had changed hands three times in as many years) and immediately began running the kinds of promotions that hadn't been used much before in our area. He held all-night tent sales and brought in clowns and ponies on weekends to entertain the kids. Promotion was the key thrust in his marketing strategy.

ANECDOTE 4: Finally, a business owner I know of wanted to sell teddies and other lingerie items. But instead of trying to crack the already crowded traditional outlets for teddies, lingerie shops and catalogs, he chose a unique new place in which to offer teddies— truck stops. His reasoning was that truckers and traveling salesmen would buy teddies on impulse as gifts for their wives or girlfriends.

The focus of his marketing plan was where he sold his products—in other words, place.

FOUR AREAS YOU CAN CONTROL

If you think about it, there are really just four basic areas over which most businesses, especially small businesses, have any direct control. And, perhaps even more important from a marketing standpoint, these are the four areas in which they can hope to achieve uniqueness over the competition. In marketing, these areas are known as the Four Ps: price, product, promotion, and place.

Of course, there are all sorts of other elements that can have a profound impact on the small-business owner, including the number and relative strength of competitors, laws and/or government regulations, the state of the general economy, technology, and the changing demographics and/or lifestyles of customers. Small-business owners may try to influence some of these elements: for instance, by writing letters to their legislators to support some proposed law. But, at best, the influence is indirect.

Although all of the Four Ps are always present and operating in all businesses, one of the four usually emerges as the key element in a business's marketing program.

It has been my experience that the new business operator who does not have a background in marketing often tends to focus on one or two of the Four Ps, and to give little, if any, thought to the other two or three. Sometimes, if the business owner is smart, or lucky, he or she will pick the key one to focus on. Unfortunately, too often this isn't the case.

I want to emphasize this point because it is an important one. The Four Ps are universal and fundamental. They govern every business, big or small. Because they are so universal and fundamental, they are often overlooked or taken for granted. Although all of the Four Ps affect every business to some degree or another, for individual businesses, one of the four usually ends up as the pivotal element in marketing planning. Recognizing which is the key element and giving it the attention it deserves may be the most critical decision a business operator can make.

A warning: My discussion of the Four Ps here is highly oversimplified. It is intended to introduce the concept to those who do not have a marketing background. A discussion of the Four Ps that would be thorough enough to cover every business is far beyond the scope of this book. What I hope is that this brief overview will serve as a catalyst, stimulate your thinking, and motivate you to do any needed follow-up research.

Let's briefly explore the Four Ps to see how they work together and why you should give some thought to each of them, especially if you're in a start-up mode.

Price

Price is what you charge for your product or service. Some might argue that in our highly competitive, price-oriented marketplace, it is the most important marketing decision you can make. I'm not sure I would necessarily agree. It seems to me that precisely because the marketplace is so price-driven, the really savvy small-business marketer would want to look for ways to get off the price-cutting merry-go-round and find another way to compete.

First, you need to give some thought to which general price category you want to be in: low, moderate, or high. Make no mistake about it: The price category in which you operate is by no means a given. It is your choice.

Rule of thumb: The lower the price category you are in, the more competitors you will have. This seems odd, since you'd think that most businesses would just love to charge top dollar for their products or services. Yet, for some reason, few choose the high price category as their niche.

In fact, for most small businesses, choosing a moderate or even higher price category may be the wisest choice. Why? For one thing, because most small businesses simply do not have the buying power and/or backup resources to play price games with the mass merchandisers—it's a little like a go-cart trying to race a formula car. For another, the small business can justify a moderate or even high price by giving value-added services that mass merchandisers can't.

Second, you need to determine what your actual marketplace price will be, which, ironically, has relatively little to do with what it actually costs to produce a product or service. Now, I recognize that that's a horrible oversimplification; the cost of materials, labor, promotions, and the level of profit you want will all have an impact on what you charge. But we might say that these elements determine the base price, the lowest price at which you can sell your product or service without losing money. That may or may not have anything to do with the market price.

In fact, it's my experience that most marketers try to set their initial prices too low, falling into the Price Is Everything trap (see Chapter 2). It's always easier to lower prices than to raise them. If you're going to lean one way or the other, lean toward starting with a higher price, because you can always discount (cut your price) later if you have to.

Of course, you must first determine your base price. A business owner I'm acquainted with went into the marketplace without having done this. Only after two years of frustration did the owner finally figure out that for many of the company's products, it was actually costing the company more to make each item than it was charging for it. Needless to say, that company is no longer in business.

Once you've determined your base price, you should begin to look for ways to add value to your product or service so that you can charge more than the minimum for it—things like:

- No charge for setup or assembly: For example, a bike shop might put together your new bike for you.
- Follow-up support: For instance, a computer retailer might answer phoned-in questions for up to a year after the sale.
- An extended warranty, say doubling the manufacturer's warranty period for free service.
- A no-questions-asked satisfaction guarantee, a la Land's End's famous GUARANTEED. PERIOD.
- A service department that's open on weekends and/or evenings.

Product

Your product is what you specifically offer for sale to your customers. By the way, always keep in mind that in marketing, "product" is defined in the broadest context; a service is just as much a product as a tangible object.

Some businesses do actually control all the elements of their product. They design it and make it; they are the inventor and manufacturer. But these are the minority. Most businesses inherit their products or services ready-made in one form or another from a supplier.

No matter which category you fall into, the specific decisions you make about your individual product(s) are complex; it takes a real juggling act to balance all the seeming trade-offs. A couple of small illustrations:

Let's say you intend to manufacture something—it really doesn't matter what. Should you make your products out of the highest-quality materials, so that they will last a long time but will cost more? Or should you compromise a little on materials, so that you'll be able to offer them at a lower cost? Should you finish them completely, which will require you to make lots of them in different colors and therefore have lots of money tied up in inventory? Or should you offer them unfinished and let the buyers do what they want, saving you warehousing and inventory costs? Should you stamp them, which is cheaper and faster and allows you to make more at less cost? Or should you forge them, which is more time-consuming and costly, but also makes a stronger product?

Or let's say you're going to open a retail store. Should you deal only in well-recognized and heavily advertised brand names, which usually cost more? Or should you go for off brands or even generics that you can offer at a lower price? For that matter, should you go "exclusive" with one well-respected and well-known brand, say the industry leader? Or should you stock several brands, including head-to-head competitors? Should you stock a manufacturer's entire line, from the smallest size to the biggest? Or should you specialize in just petites or just big and tall?

As involved as your specific product decisions might seem to be, from a marketing standpoint they all boil down to one critical question: What do your intended customers want that they are not getting now? While this ought to be as obvious as the fact that the sun came up this morning, in my experience with small businesses, it sometimes isn't.

Unfortunately, what too often happens is that the entrepreneur gets seduced by a product's gee-whiz bells and whistles and loses sight of what the ultimate customer wants and/or needs. This is another one of those fundamentals that is so basic that it is taken for granted. But it shouldn't be.

Every decision you make about your product, whether you design and manufacture it yourself or intend to buy it ready-made from someone else, should be guided—no, I'll use an even stronger term; should be driven—by the needs of the ultimate customer in your marketplace.

The irony of it is, if you really do buy into allowing the needs of your customers to drive your product decisions, the juggling act of trying to balance all those seemingly contradictory trade-offs really becomes a lot easier to handle.

Promotion

How you promote your business is what this book and its companion publications, *Do-It-Yourself Publicity* and *Do-It-Yourself Advertising*, are all about. Earlier I said that some people think that price may be the most important of the Four Ps, but that I disagreed. If I were to nominate a candidate for the most critical of the Four Ps, especially for small businesses, I think it would be promotion.

The most important thing any small business must do to survive in today's highly competitive marketplace is to establish its uniqueness in the minds of its customers and potential customers. This is a theme that will appear again and again in this book; in fact, it is the subject of a chapter all by itself. It is a fundamental theme of the other two books as well.

Think about this for a moment. You might be the nicest folks in town. You might have the best products and the most economical prices. You might be located in the most convenient spot. However, if no one knows that you have these things and no one recognizes your superiority to your competitors, then your business is doomed—remember the Better Mousetrap myth?

The fact is, virtually every business, whether it's a small local retailer or a national manufacturer, has a vast arsenal of promotional "weapons" to choose from: paid advertising in all sorts of media, free publicity in all sorts of media, direct mail, personal sales calls, trade shows, point-of-sale displays, sponsoring special events, celebrity endorsements. Even the packaging of your product or how you decorate your store is an element of promotion.

The fact is, most small businesses can't afford to (nor, for that matter, do they need to) use all these weapons. A neighborhood mom-and-pop convenience store does not need to "nuke 'em" by advertising on network TV.

Rather, in promoting your business, the key is to find which weapon works for you, in your marketplace, in your competitive situation, and given your customer group.

Place

If I were going to nominate the one of the Four Ps that most generally gets short shrift in small-business marketing planning, it would be place.

Place is essentially where your end customer will find your product or service. Depending on what business you're in, there are two kinds of place decision:

1. For the business that sells its products or services directly to the general public, place is where the business is physically located—in a mall, on a busy street, in a prestige office building.
2. For the business that does not sell directly to the end customer, the "place" decision becomes how it will distribute its products or services so that they are available to the general consumer.

Let's look at each one briefly.

For the business that sells directly to the general consumer, the place decision usually ends up being a compromise among three key elements:

1. Affordability for the business—in other words, how much the business can afford to pay in rent or to own a building.
2. The image of the location; for example, an exclusive dress shop wouldn't want to locate in a slum.
3. Convenience for the customer, such as access to a main thoroughfare, having adequate adjacent parking, and being near other shopping.

Of necessity, for many capital-poor small businesses, affordability ends up being the determining element. But the other two should at least be given some careful thought.

On balance, I think the place decision for the business that plans to sell its products or services indirectly is a tougher one. Virtually every industry has some kind of distribution system. These systems have evolved over the years and have generally been in place for a long time. Each industry seems to have its own unique rules and procedures, which sometimes (often?) involve idiosyncrasies that may trace their origins to centuries-old practices, but seem to make no sense in today's world. You are not going to change them easily. They are a given. If you want to be part of the system, you have to learn what that system's rules are and play by them.

To make matters even worse, distributors do not like to handle new products. Think about the basic nature of their business and you'll understand why. A distributor's basic need is to move products through the system; in other words, the business is volume driven. The more units moved, the more money the distributor makes. This is why distributors want proven winners in the marketplace, and why they tend to avoid new products that are untried and unproven. It's true, your new product might ultimately prove to be a real marketplace winner; if it is, the distributor will then say, "Come see me."

So, you might think, if the distribution system is so hard to break into, I'll just bypass it and take my product direct to the consumer. I'll advertise in magazines and send out direct mailers, and people can order from me directly. That way I'll make even more money, since I won't have to share it with a bunch of middlemen.

This, of course, has been tried countless times by countless businesses, usually with little success. There are two reasons for this.

First, the distribution system works because it ultimately delivers the product to where the consumer wants to buy it and to where the customer is used to looking for it. Don't ever underestimate the importance of that.

Second, from a marketing standpoint, you can't afford to reinvent the wheel, which is in effect what you're trying to do by bypassing the distribution system. As countless small businesses have discovered, much to their chagrin, most single ads in magazines and most direct mail campaigns do *not* generate enough direct orders to even pay for the cost of the ad or mailer. Unless the small business is unusually well heeled (and I haven't yet found one that is), it simply can't afford the upfront market development costs involved in bypassing the distributor system.

Getting Started Tomorrow Morning

Sit back for a moment and think about your business. Jot down some notes if you like.

Which of the Four Ps has been dominant in the marketing of your individual business? There is no answer that's either right or wrong in all cases. It's whatever's right for you, in your marketplace, given your resources and the nature of your competition.

Go with your first-blush answer. Do you think it's the one that should have been dominant? If not, which one would you now elevate in importance?

Think about price: Which pricing category do you fall into, low, moderate, or high? How have you traditionally determined your pricing? Do you set your own prices or simply follow the competition? What pricing category are most of your competitors in? Have you (or they) fallen into the Price-Is-Everything trap? Could there be a marketplace opportunity in a different pricing category? What could you do to add value and therefore justify a higher price?

Think about product: Be honest now. Haven't you made product decisions that have been governed more by your convenience (you cut the number of sizes you carry to save inventory costs, you hired less experienced people to save salary costs, you replaced some stronger metal parts with plastic because you could cut manufacturing costs by a few pennies) than by what your customers want? The truth is, in business, compromises are a given. The critical question is: Which side has been dominant, your convenience or marketplace desires?

Think about promotion: If you're like most small-business owners, especially if your company is a start-up, you've probably given relatively little thought to the specifics of how you're going to promote your business. Am I right? Haven't you tended to buy into the Better Mousetrap myth, sort of expecting the world to beat a path to your door? Haven't you tended to lump all advertising media together as more or less interchangeable? Haven't you tended to put marketing, advertising, and promotion decisions into the "when I have time for it" category?

Think about place: Indeed, how much real thought have you given to your place decisions? If you're selling direct to the consumer, which element was dominant in picking a location, affordability, image, or customer convenience? Which one should have been? If you're selling indirectly, how many distributors in your industry have you talked to? Do you even know who the major distributors are?

4

Target (Niche) Marketing in the 1990s

My father was a duck hunter. Duck hunters go out in the cold and sit quietly in a duck blind alongside a river or lake holding their shotguns for long periods of time. And they wait. And wait. And wait some more. It takes a lot of patience to be a good duck hunter.

It also takes more than patience. If you think about it, duck hunters have to make a lot of rather specialized decisions in order to be successful. For example:

They have to artistically design a duck blind so that from a flying duck's point of view, it looks like a natural part of the landscape. No flashing neon signs saying, "Ducks Land Here!"

They have to carefully pick a location that ducks are likely to use, perhaps near food or a protected backwater. It's not likely to be near an interstate highway or have paved parking adjacent.

They put out plastic or wooden decoy ducks and use funny-sounding duck calls in an effort to attract ducks. They don't want robins or bluejays or even pheasants to stop by—just ducks.

And they wait until the ducks are within range before firing their shotguns. No blasting away at anything that flies as it passes overhead.

Now, you might ask, what does duck hunting have to do with marketing?

It provides a good analogy to help introduce a fundamental concept of modern marketing. In fact, this concept is so basic that it is often overlooked or taken for granted by the small marketer. This is a serious mistake. Virtually every decision the small marketer makes in marketing his or her product should be governed by this all-important concept. Indeed, it is only through a thorough understanding of this basic concept that the small marketer can hope to successfully compete not only with other small marketers, but with the industry giants as well. It is an idea we have touched on or alluded to obliquely several times already, but we will now look at it in its own right.

It is the concept of target or niche marketing. Those who have already read *Do-It-Yourself Advertising* will recognize that this chapter parallels the chapter in that book called "Fragmentation and Targeting," although it comes at the topic from a somewhat different angle.

NOT EVERY BIRD IS A TARGET

Let's return to our duck hunter analogy for a moment. Remember, the duck hunter only wants to shoot at ducks. The duck hunter doesn't want to shoot robins or seagulls or other kinds of nongame birds because they are not good eating. The duck hunter does not want to shoot pheasants because they are probably not in season. The duck hunter certainly does not want to shoot eagles because it is against the law. In other words, not every bird that flies is a potential target for the duck hunter. Quite literally, the target market is ducks and only ducks. In fact, we might even extend this analogy and say that the duck hunter's family has told the hunter that they only like to eat mallards, not to bother shooting any other kind of duck! Now that's a niche.

In the same way, the concept of target or niche marketing says that not everyone in a given market universe is a likely or even necessarily a potential customer. By the way, in marketing, "universe" simply means however you designate your market size. For some businesses, like Ford Motor Company or Campbell Soup, the entire world is the market universe. For others, say a local car dealer, the universe might be a county and perhaps parts of an adjacent county or two. And for a small convenience store, the universe might be no more than the nearby neighborhood.

FROM MASS MARKETING TO NICHE MARKETING

In the decades following World War II, large national companies, like Procter & Gamble or Sears Roebuck, marketed their products, like Tide laundry detergent or Craftsman tools, to what were called mass markets. These markets were usually numbered in the tens of millions and tended to be defined in broad, almost stereotypical categories: the housewife, the businessman, the blue-collar worker.

These marketers used the mass media, network TV and radio and large-circulation magazines, which also measured their audiences in the millions and even tens of millions, to reach these markets.

In the 1970s, as marketers used market research to learn more and more about their markets, a major transition began that has remade the face of modern marketing. In their efforts to gain a competitive marketplace edge, sophisticated marketers discovered that the large mass markets they were gearing their products and promotions for actually had lots of submarkets, or niche markets.

For example, the housewife consumer category wasn't just the still-in-the-home suburban-mother-of-two traditionally depicted in ads. The housewife category could also include a working mother, a single mother, and a childless wife, which, in turn, could be broken down into a younger newly married wife and an older empty-nester wife. Marketers discovered that the real people in these niche markets tended to have specialized needs and that by developing and promoting products that would appeal to just these specific needs, they could get a competitive marketplace edge.

In other words, a marketing Pandora's box was opened, leading to all kinds of product fragmentation, audience fragmentation, and media fragmentation. Let's explore each of these in a bit more detail from a local marketer's perspective.

Product Fragmentation

As an illustration of how product fragmentation might work at the local level, all we have to do is take a look at the typical shopping mall. Have you ever counted how many places there are to buy blue jeans at a typical mall?

There are usually at least a couple of department stores, one of which displays upscale or designer jeans, the other standard name brands, generally at about half the price.

There are typically at least half a dozen jean specialty shops. One might push "trendy" jeans for junior and senior high school students. Another might specialize in western jeans. A third might carry mostly "relaxed fit" jeans, which is an industry code word for adult. A fourth might be selling large-size jeans. A fifth might carry just its own "fashion" brand. And a sixth might be an "off-price" shop, offering name-brand jeans at discount prices.

Then, on top of these (by the way, if you're counting, we're already up to eight places where you can buy jeans), there are generally half a dozen more clothing shops that, although they specialize in other items, carry a limited selection of blue jeans. Maybe they offer only imported brands of jeans or jeans in colors other than the traditional indigo blue.

In other words, there may be a dozen or more different places in which to buy blue jeans, each trying to stand for something different to the consumer—to occupy a unique position relative to other jean shops in the mind of a potential customer. Which jean shop that customer will choose depends on his or her perceived needs at the time.

Product fragmentation is, therefore, a conscious effort by a marketer to differentiate his or her product or service from other similar products or services in the marketplace.

Audience Fragmentation

In effect, this is the opposite side of the same coin. Whereas product fragmentation is based on qualities inherent in the products or services, in audience fragmentation we focus on factors inherent in each group that distinguish it from some other group.

The price the marketer charges for his or her product is probably the biggest single factor that differentiates audience segments. For some buyers, there are three factors involved in the buy decision: price, price, and price! They will buy something only if it's on sale and will drive across town to save pennies. For others, only the "best" will do, and price is no object. The quality inherent in the consumer here is his or her perception of his or her monetary resources (limited or plentiful) and need for a certain product (one's need may simply be to buy a pair of utilitarian jeans in which to go to work, whereas another's need might be to make a fashion statement in order to win acceptance).

Some other factors that distinguish one target group from another at the local level are geography or location, which usually translates into convenience, age, and lifestyle.

Media Fragmentation

And then there are the media, which have been blasted into umpteen smithereens, even at the local level.

Once most of us could get three local over-the-air TV stations representing the three major networks. Now we can flip through three dozen or more cable channels, and more than a hundred if we have a satellite dish.

Once we only needed to choose from five or six local AM radio stations, of which one usually dominated the teen market and another controlled the adult market. Now, in addition to those traditional AM stations, there are a half dozen more FM stations, which have virtually taken over the music formats.

Most of us grew up reading our hometown newspaper, either a daily or a weekly. It was the only paper you took. (Well, maybe some intellectuals also took a big-city Sunday paper, but they were the exception.) Now, in addition to that hometown paid subscription newspaper, there are now probably one or more free-circulation shoppers, one or more classified ad papers, a senior citizens tabloid, a singles paper, maybe a business publication, maybe a labor weekly, and maybe an entertainment or tourist-oriented "magazine."

There has been an explosion in the number of trade publications in just about any industry you can name. Once upon a time there was generally one paid subscription magazine or newspaper that "owned" an entire industry. Today, while the leader may still be around and may still be in the lead, its lead has probably been whittled away by a half dozen or more free magazines or tabloid newspapers, each focusing on a specialized niche within the industry.

In other words, just a few years ago a local marketer might have felt overwhelmed if he or she had even a dozen possible choices for advertising. Today's small advertiser, confronted by a veritable parade of salespeople representing literally scores of different advertising vehicles, would be relieved if he or she had to deal with "only" a dozen media reps.

PICK YOUR TARGETS TO SURVIVE

The basic premise behind the concept of niche or target marketing is that no one marketer can be all things to all people. Even the big boys aren't immune; just think about what's happened to Sears Roebuck and General Motors in the 1980s and 1990s. If the big boys, with their deep pockets and marketing sophistication, are vulnerable, imagine how tough it is for the little guy!

There are factors inherent in the products or services you offer—for example, their positioning—that automatically limit their appeal. There are factors inherent in your customer universe, such as lifestyle, age, or location, that mean that certain products or services will be of value to them and others will not. There are factors inherent in the media that limit your ability to reach people with your ad message.

And, perhaps most important of all, there is the intense competition inherent in today's marketplace. Everyone has head-to-head competition: Hardee's, Wendy's, and Burger King are going head-to-head with McDonald's in the hamburger business. And everyone has lots of indirect competitors or substitutes: Rocky Roccoco, Taco Bell, and Popeye's, as well as Oscar Mayer Lunchables and made-at-home peanut butter and jelly sandwiches, are all substitutes for a trip to McDonald's.

What all this boils down to is this: No small business, nonprofit organization, or volunteer group has the resources to be all things to all people. You simply have no choice but to focus, to target your marketing efforts on a limited number of identifiable groups.

Who do you focus your marketing efforts on? That's easy: the most likely buyer of your products or services. This is the logical extension of everything that I've been talking about in this chapter. The interplay of all these factors means that there are one or more groups of people who are much more likely to be your customers than others.

The key to success in today's marketplace is to identify those groups as specifically as you can and to focus everything you do to market your business, especially your paid media advertising, to them.

Getting Started Tomorrow Morning

Get out a legal pad or piece of notebook paper. As best you can, answer each of the following questions in twenty-five words or less. Don't worry about style; the idea here is just to start thinking along these lines.

- What's your position in the marketplace? In other words, what do your customers think of your business? And make no mistake about it, you do have a unique and specific position.
- Who are your most likely buyers? If you think you appeal to more than one group, you can give each twenty-five words of description. If you do have more than one group of most likely buyers, can you prioritize them as to their importance to you?
- Finally, off the top of your head, list all the media in your community. List those that are based in or specifically focus on your community or area. Think broadly. Don't limit yourself to the traditional media: daily or weekly newspapers, radio stations, and TV stations. Think about all the other kinds of local media people rely on for certain kinds of information.

5

Establishing
Your Uniqueness

The perceptive reader will have already guessed where this is headed. If there are all these competitors out there, vying for the attention and, therefore, the dollars of customers, then for any individual business or organization to survive, it is absolutely critical that that business or organization establish its uniqueness in the marketplace.

There is a fundamental law in physics that says that two objects cannot occupy the same space at the same time. That law is equally basic to marketing: In the perceptions of customers, two organizations cannot occupy the same space at the same time.

We are not talking here about physical occupancy. Rather, we are talking about who the marketplace thinks you are, your identity in the minds of customers and potential customers. In other words, we are talking about your image.

In any given category of purchases and in any given marketplace, there can be only one business occupying each niche.

Here's what I'm trying to suggest: If you were to approach ten different consumers and ask them to name the lowest price place or the top-of-the-line place or the most selection place for the purchase of men's clothing in your marketplace, you might get ten different answers for each niche; in other words, each customer, for various reasons, might perceive a different place as the lowest-price place or the top-of-the-line place. But I'd be willing to bet that you would get only one answer per niche.

THE NICHES

Ironically, there are only six basic niches that any business can occupy:

1. *The lowest price/lowest quality.* This is the place where the consumer thinks he or she will consistently find the cheapest price on any given category of purchases. And in most consumers' minds, the lowest price almost always means the lowest quality as well.

Some national marketers are trying to stake out a compromise position: that they have the lowest prices, yet good quality. However, the price equals quality equation is deeply ingrained in the psyche of the marketplace and is going to be very hard to change.

2. *The highest price/best quality (or top of the line).* This is the opposite side of the same coin. It is the place where the consumer perceives that he or she will get the best in any given purchase category, and will, consequently, pay the highest price.

There are a number of national marketers who have specifically positioned their products as the best and, therefore, the highest priced in the category. In automobiles, for most people it's probably the Rolls Royce, and for watches, it's probably the Rolex.

3. *The most selection.* This is the place where the consumer perceives that he or she will find the most variety in any given purchase category. Prices are generally in the moderate range.

Today's superstores, which generally offer many different brands of the same basic types of products, are examples of businesses that are positioned as having the most selection.

4. *The best service.* This is the place where customers feel "they really take care of you," according to how being taken care of is defined in any given purchase category.

Some national marketers are trying to get a toehold in this position by promoting service, but it remains a particularly excellent one for small and/or locally owned businesses that are trying to compete effectively with the "big boys."

5. *The friendliest.* This is the place where consumers expect to get the nicest treatment.

This position is getting lots of attention these days, especially among large national marketers, with their emphasis on good customer service. However, like the best service niche, it is one where the small and/or locally owned business will almost always have the stronger position.

6. *The most convenient.* This is the place where the customer perceives that it is easiest to make a purchase in any given category. In most cases this means geographic proximity to where the con-

sumer either works or lives, but it can also mean convenience in how the shop is laid out or that it provides free pickup and delivery.

Once in a great while a business is fortunate enough to occupy more than one niche at the same time. For example, the top of the line place might also be the best service place or the friendliest place. This is, of course, a very desirable achievement, since occupying more than one niche puts that business in a very strong market position.

But I would also suggest that this is the exception rather than the rule. For most consumers, any given business can occupy only one niche at a time.

YOU DON'T HAVE A CHOICE; YOU MUST CHOOSE!

As a marketer you don't have a choice. A business *must* be something in the minds of its customers. You can either choose your niche consciously or let the marketplace choose it for you. As a marketer you have, in effect, just two choices:

1. If yours is a new business, you can either move into an unoccupied niche in the marketplace or try to dislodge someone from an existing niche.
2. If yours is an existing business, you can either defend the niche you presently occupy or try to move into another one, in which case you are acting like yours is a new business.

The New Business

As the owner of a new business, it is very much to your advantage to seek out and move into an unoccupied niche in the marketplace, rather than trying to replace someone who is already occupying a niche. For one thing, from a promotional standpoint it is much easier to establish a new identity than it is to try to take someone else's away. This also translates into being much less expensive.

If, however, after carefully analyzing the marketplace, you conclude that there isn't an unoccupied niche available, then you should go after whoever is most vulnerable. You do not want to try to dislodge the market leader, which is, after all, in the strongest position to defend itself.

The Established Business

As the owner of an existing business, your first choice, hands down, should always be to defend your present position. If your business has an established place in the marketplace, then you, in effect, control the high ground. It is both easier and far less expensive.

Unfortunately, marketplaces change and the needs of customers change. Established businesses that don't recognize these changes often can become vulnerable to being dislodged by a newcomer.

The most dangerous position of all for the owner of an established business, however, is not knowing what niche the business occupies. Then you are really vulnerable to having someone dislodge it from its position.

YOU *MUST* ESTABLISH YOUR UNIQUENESS

The point of this chapter is one that you're going to see me hammer at again and again throughout this book: Your business *must* establish its uniqueness in the marketplace. You *don't* have a choice about that. It is the key to survival.

The concept of establishing uniqueness is what drives all of the following chapters. Think about it: The fundamental goal behind all forms of promotion, whether paid advertising or direct mail, whether in-store banners or a special event, is to establish the unique position of your business in the minds of your customers or potential customers.

Getting Started Tomorrow Morning

If yours is an established business, what *is* its position in your marketplace? Which *one* of the six positions have you staked out for it? Yes, I know; you've spent lots of money telling everyone that your business has top quality, that its prices are competitive, that it delivers excellent service, that its people are friendly, and that it's conveniently located. Yawn.

Make no mistake about it, the marketing reality is that a business cannot occupy all of those positions at the same time. One of them is dominant in the minds of your customers. So, be real honest: Which *one* image have you consistently given priority to over the years?

If yours is a new business, which *one* of the above positions do you think is available in the marketplace, either because no one occupies it at present or because the business that presently occupies it is not defending it well and is, therefore, vulnerable?

Now, the second key question for the new business owner: Is this niche one that you are qualified to occupy by experience and/or talent?

6

Choosing a Name for Your Business

At first glance, choosing a name for your business might seem like a simple, straightforward task: You just pick something you like and go with it. But, in fact, it is something you need to give a great deal of thought and consideration to, both from a marketing standpoint and for the legal implications.

From a marketing standpoint, picking your business name may be one of the most critical decisions you can make. Your business name is how people know who you are. It is how the business is identified. Seeing its name is probably the very first impression people have about your business—and we all know how important first impressions can be.

Think about it for a moment. The first time you hear the name of a new business, don't you form an almost instantaneous impression of that business?

1. You obviously get some important information about what kind of business it is. Joe's Tire Mart certainly isn't the same business as Mary's Intimate Apparel.
2. You probably also immediately think of that business in terms of your own needs and wants. If you like Mexican food, hearing about a new place called Juan's Taco House goes into a mental file that says, "Try this place." But if you're not a seafood fan, being told that John's Lobster House just opened probably gets shuffled into the "Who cares?" category.

3. When you hear the name of a business, you are also likely to form an instantaneous first impression about its style of doing business and whether you'd be comfortable going there. For example, if you're basically a blue jeans and flannel shirt person, you're probably not going to rush over to a new shop that calls itself Elite Clothiers for Men. But you may very well plan to attend the grand opening of Jeans Galore.

You see, picking a business name isn't quite as easy as you thought. We'll have more to say about the marketing implications of picking a business name in a minute. But first we need to look at least briefly at some of the legal aspects of picking a business name.

GET PROFESSIONAL ADVICE

The name of this book—*Do-It-Yourself Marketing*—notwithstanding, this is one of the areas where it's definitely wise to secure professional help.

I am not an attorney, and I certainly do not want to even come close to giving legal advice here. But you need to understand that choosing and establishing a business name has some very important legal implications. Involve professional legal counsel in the process of deciding on a name for your business. It can save you from lots of potentially very expensive problems down the road.

For one thing, most states and many counties and municipalities have laws and/or rules and regulations that affect your use of a business name. These laws and/or rules and regulations can vary significantly from area to area, ranging from a basically hands-off policy that allows you to do just about anything you want to some very restrictive policies that may require registration and/or licensing before you can operate.

For another thing, if you are going to do business across state lines, numerous—and very complex—federal laws and/or rules and regulations may come into play, depending on what kind of business you're in.

You need to find someone who is knowledgeable about these federal, state, and local laws and/or rules and regulations.

Then, besides being conscientious about meeting any local, state, or federal requirements, there is the whole issue of making sure you have not selected a name that is similar to the name of an existing business in the marketplace you want to serve. There are trademark laws and other legal protections for someone that has already established use of a business name.

What a disaster it would be to find out, after you've spent thousands of dollars to promote your new business, that its name is too much like that of another business. The very least that could happen would be that you would have to stop using the name you had already promoted, in effect sending you back to square one. Worse, there might be a lawsuit for damages.

Finally, there's the other side of the same coin. You need to consult an attorney in order to make sure that you've adequately protected your business name, so that no one else can use it.

IT'S ALSO BAD MARKETING

Even if you could conceivably come up with a name that is similar to that of another business, but that would pass a legal test, this is just plain bad marketing.

You never, ever want to pick a name that is close to that of another business. I know the temptation is sometimes there: "We'll just piggyback on their recognition." But using a name that is similar to or suggestive of the name of an already established business actually reinforces that business.

There is an even more subtle trap that many owners of small start-up businesses fall into: Coming up with a name that, while different enough to escape any legal problems, sounds similar enough to others in the marketplace to do nothing to establish the new business's uniqueness.

Here's an oversimplified example of what I mean. Suppose there already is a Joe's Wrecker Service, a Bob's Towing Service, and a Smith and Son Towing in your community. If you come along and call your business Ted's Tow Truck, you probably won't have any legal problems, as long as your name is Ted. However, from a marketing standpoint, you've chosen a very weak name. Because it is so similar to all the others, you've done nothing to establish your uniqueness.

How do you get around this? Here are a couple of suggestions. If the names of most other businesses follow one style or approach, go in a different direction. For example, Ted might choose to call his business Ted's 24-Hour Wrecker Service or Ted's Quick Response Wrecker or Ted's Go Anywhere Towing Service. Even though the others will, in fact, do twenty-four-hour towing, respond quickly, and go anywhere, Ted's the one who's put it right there in his name for everyone to see.

STEP ONE TOWARD UNIQUENESS

In Chapter 5 I went to some lengths to stress the importance of establishing uniqueness in the marketplace. In a very real sense, picking a name for your business is step one in the process of differentiating your business from the competition.

We touched briefly on some of the marketing implications of choosing a business name at the beginning of this chapter. Now let's look at them more closely.

First, always say what you do in your business name. If your business is a hardware store, say so. If it's an insurance agency, say so. If it's a dog walking service, say so.

If you don't say what your business does, then it won't be anything in the minds of potential customers. This is very important, particularly for new businesses.

Certainly you can think of dozens of examples of successful businesses that have ignored this advice, whose business names include no hint as to what they do. But I'd also bet that most of these would be businesses that have been around for a while.

What I'm trying to suggest here is that with a new business trying to enter today's highly competitive marketplace, you'll be just that much further ahead in establishing its identity if you include a clear statement of what kind of business it is in the name.

Second, think about what you want to say about your business with a name. What image do you want to project? What niche do you want to occupy in the marketplace?

Consider using a descriptive word in your business name that clearly establishes the niche you're after.

If you want your business to be known for the quality of its work or products, then suggest that image right in the name: Quality Home Improvement, Custom Crafted Woodworking, Blue Ribbon Beauty Salon, Elite Men's Wear.

If you want it to be known for its low prices, then say so: Discount Office Supplies, Value Shoes, Pay Less Car Mart, Bargain Furniture Center.

If you want it to be known for its personal service and friendliness, then suggest this in the name: Personal Touch Flowers, Friendly Barber Shop, Hometown Heating & Air Conditioning.

Sell Yourself

Using your own name in your business name can have some real advantages.

For one thing, it *is* your name. This means that in most cases no one else can use it, since you already "own" it. However, this is one of those areas where you should consult professional legal advice before you make any final decisions.

Using your own name can also be a major asset if you're already well known. For instance, if you were a star athlete, a well-known entertainer, or even someone prominent in the community for any reason, building on that existing name recognition factor can give you a real head start in establishing your uniqueness.

Using your own name in your business name can also help to establish the all-important sense of a personal relationship with customers. This can be one of the major strengths of a small business competing with the "big boys."

Think about it for a minute. Especially at the local level, people don't usually think of themselves as doing business with a business. Rather, they think of themselves as doing business with a trusted friend. If the car is running rough, they don't say, "Let's take it down to Nick's Auto Service." Chances are it's more like, "I'm gonna take it over to Nick; maybe he can do something with it."

In other words, people like to do business with people. Why not

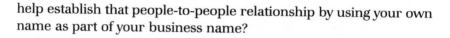

help establish that people-to-people relationship by using your own name as part of your business name?

Have Some Fun

Most business names are very serious; some even border on being outright stuffy. Why not buck the trend and establish your uniqueness in the marketplace with some humor?

For example, if you're going to start an appliance repair service, don't be plain old Joe's Appliance Repair. Who cares? There must be half a dozen appliance repair places listed in the phone book. Instead, why not call your business The Appliance Doctor? It clearly establishes what you do and is certainly memorable. If you're going to start a delivery service, instead of being Middletown Delivery Service (yawn), why not call your business Speedy Delivery and establish your niche as the delivery service that hustles?

Getting Started Tomorrow Morning

If you haven't already picked a name for your business, sit down and brainstorm some ideas.

Except, if I know small entrepreneurs, the chances are that you've already got a sheet of notebook paper covered with a couple of dozen or more different names.

Take each name and grade it according to the following criteria. For each criterion, award the name from 1 to 5 points; 5 points means you think the name does a very good job of meeting the criterion, and 1 point means it is really weak in that category.

1. Does the name include a specific suggestion of what kind of business it is, what it does?   _____

2. Does the name give a clear indication of what niche the business intends to occupy?   _____

3. Does the name have a friendly, personal feel? Or does it make use of humor or fun in any way?   _____

4. Is the name clearly different from the names of others doing similar things in the mar-

ketplace? (Award yourself double points for this
one—10 is tops.)

                                   TOTAL POINTS   _____

There are a total of 25 possible points:

- If your prospective name got fewer than 10 points, forget it.
  From a marketing standpoint, it's weak.
- If it got between 13 and 19 points, and especially if adjust-
  ments will give it more marketing strength, it's a possibility.
- If your name got 20 or more points, you've got a winner.

7

Designing Your Own Logo

I can certainly understand how the owner of a new business that is just getting started might not have gotten around to designing a logo, although I do think this is a case of mistaken priorities. But it never ceases to amaze me when I find well-established businesses that don't have a consistent logo.

The name of the business appears in a different style of type every time it runs an ad—sometimes it's all caps, sometimes it's upper and lower case; sometimes it's Old English and sometimes it's Avant Garde. And it's different on the letterhead and on the envelopes, and both are different from the way it appears on shipping labels. And the name appears in yet another form on the side of the delivery truck.

Talk about a schizophrenic identity.

MISTAKEN PRIORITIES

I would suggest that having a unique logo for your business or organization is *not* one of those when-we-have-time or when-we-can-afford-it projects. On the contrary, it is a top priority, ranking alongside finding a suitable location for your business, ordering your supplies, and arranging for your phone system.

In fact, if I were to write a Marketing Ten Commandments, near the top of the list would be, "Thou shalt have a unique logo and insist on its use!" Use it on everything—ads, letterhead and envelopes, signs, vehicles, and even the uniforms your people wear.

Think about it. The name of your business is how people identify it. It's what they remember about your business, and it's how they refer to it when talking to their friends and colleagues. You want the name of your business or organization to be quickly recognized and easily remembered. A set logo, consistently used, will enhance that recognition and recall factor many times over.

Major advertisers have long known about the marketing power of a unique logo. To illustrate my point, here's a quickie quiz to see if you can match the familiar graphic symbol on the left with the correct major corporation on the right:

1. A bell ___	A. Allstate Insurance
2. A five-pointed star inside a pentagram ___	B. Mercedes Benz
	C. McDonald's
3. A seashell ___	D. Apple Computer
4. Cupped hands ___	E. John Deere
5. A three-pointed star inside a circle ___	F. Prudential Insurance
	G. Shell Oil
6. A bull ___	H. American Oil Co.
7. A torch ___	I. Exxon
8. An apple ___	J. White Stag
9. The Rock of Gibraltar ___	K. Merrill Lynch
10. Clydesdale horses ___	L. The Bell companies
11. A tiger ___	M. Budweiser
12. Two crossed arches ___	N. Chrysler
13. A leaping deer ___	O. Frosted Flakes

[Answers: 1-L; 2-N; 3-G; 4-A; 5-B; 6-K; 7-H; 8-D; 9-F; 10-M; 11-I or O; 12-C; 13-E or J]

And remember, we're not talking about passing fancies here. For some of these logos we're talking about advertising and promotion that goes back thirty, forty, or even fifty years. That's consistency.

WHAT IS A LOGO?

The term *logo* comes from the word *logotype*, which dates back to hot-metal printing days. The name of a regular advertiser would have been previously set in a particular typeface. This piece of metal was kept on a shelf in the backshop. When an ad was to be set in type, the person doing the layout would put a circle or an X where the logo was to be placed and write the word "logo." The typesetter then got the logo off the shelf and dropped it in place.

In contrast, for advertisers who were not regulars, the name at the bottom of an ad was usually set in whatever typeface and style were on the Linotype machine at the time.

In the little quickie quiz above, I specifically chose graphic symbols that, through repetition and consistency, have come to be very closely associated with a specific major corporation. But a logo is not just a graphic symbol, such as a three-pointed star in a circle or the silhouette of a bell.

A logo can be defined as the name of your business appearing in a distinctive typeface or type configuration, possibly combined with a graphic element of some kind.

Thoughts on Selecting a Typeface

The common denominator for all logos is that they are set in some specific typeface or have a distinctive configuration of type. We'll talk more about what "distinctive configuration" means in a minute. But first I want to explore some thoughts on typefaces in general.

Selection of a typeface for your logo should not be taken lightly, for a number of reasons.

The first consideration when selecting a typeface for your logo is that it be easily readable. Could a commuter seeing your logo at the bottom of an ad in a newspaper or magazine being read by someone else on the other side of a train aisle read the name? Could someone whizzing past a billboard at seventy miles an hour on a freeway read the name on that billboard? Could someone who is only half paying attention to a TV show recognize your logo, even if it's only on the screen for a few seconds?

If instant recognition is one of the basic goals of having a logo, making sure it's easily readable is the means to that goal.

What this suggests is that you should tend to stay away from ornate or fancy typefaces, like Old English, script, and what are often referred to as circus types. (Examples of this latter category are the ornate type you would see on a circus poster and the frontier style you would see on a wanted poster.) These kinds of type certainly have the quality of distinctiveness, and I am not saying that you should never use them under any circumstances. I'm just saying that you need to think twice before you make them a permanent part of your logo.

The second consideration when looking for a typeface for your logo is the message the type itself is sending. There are literally thousands of typefaces. If you stop in at a full-service type shop and ask to see its type book, you'll be handed a thick notebook to look at.

And, yes, typefaces in and of themselves do carry emotional messages. Think about it a minute. Don't some typefaces suggest elegance and high class? Aren't some typefaces associated with olden times? Don't some typefaces imply high-tech, futuristic approaches? And don't some typefaces suggest delicacy and femininity and others strength and masculinity?

The feeling or message that most people associate with the typeface you select for your logo should be consistent with the image of your business that you're trying to get across. Your antique shop probably wouldn't want a logo set in a computerlike typeface. Your ladies' lingerie shop probably wouldn't want a logo set in a heavy, blocky type. Your insurance and financial services agency most likely wouldn't select a jazzy, circus-style type for a logo. A hardware store probably wouldn't want to select a thin, scriptlike typeface.

Now, what does "distinctive configuration of type" mean? It simply means that instead of using the type you select just as if it were ordinary text, you do something to it to give it even more visual distinction. Here's a quick list of some unique things you can do:

- Set the first letter oversize, in other words, in a size larger than the rest of the type. If there are several words in your business name, set the first letter of each word oversize so that it suggests the initials of your business.
- Have the type compressed, which means squeezed together, or have it elongated, which means stretched out. It's probably a good idea to compress or elongate only a little; otherwise the type will look distorted to the viewer.
- Have the type reversed, so that the letters are white against a solid background.
- Have the type italicized, which means slanted. (By the way, you can slant forward or backward.)
- Have your logo boxed, with a thin border or a heavy border. Maybe round off the corners, or round off only two of the four corners.

- Use one or more lines below and/or above the words of your logo. Maybe use lines of varying thickness.
- Stack your logo. If your business name has two or three words, try putting them one on top of the other instead of in a row.
- Slant your logo. Instead of following a horizontal or vertical orientation, try having your type run uphill at a gentle angle.
- Set all your type in lowercase, including the first letters. Or set all your type in caps except for one letter in lowercase.
- Take out the space between the letters; in other words, have them lightly touching each other.

Adding a Graphic Element

For lots of businesses, just having the name appear in a distinctive typeface or type configuration will be sufficient. However, for many businesses, the addition of some kind of graphic element is logical and desirable. A graphic element can include:

- A recognizable piece of equipment that is integral to your business—a camera for a photographer, a wineglass for a wine shop, a knife and fork for a general-line restaurant, a lobster claw for a seafood restaurant, a needle and thread for a tailor shop, a monkey wrench for a plumber, a spark plug for an auto parts shop, a comb and scissors for a barber shop.

- A shape that is closely associated with your business—a heart for a flower shop, an arrow for a delivery service, a diamond for a jewelry shop, a snowflake for a ski resort.

- A recognizable object that may not be directly associated with your business, but that still reinforces the image you're trying to get across—a rose for a lingerie shop, a lighthouse for a family counseling service, an elegant tea service for a gourmet tea and coffee shop, a vase with a whisk, spatula, and wooden spoon for a kitchen gadget shop.

- A photograph, drawing, or caricature of the business owner, especially if the owner's name is the name of the business. This is a somewhat common practice among insurance agents, financial advisers, and real estate people. It is an especially good trick to use if the business owner is highly visible in other promotions—for example, doing his or her own TV and radio ads.

• A cartoon character. Where is it written that a business always has to be stiff and formal? Maybe it does if the business is a bank or a law firm, but why couldn't an independent appliance repair service bill itself as The Appliance Doctor and use a cartoon-like character wearing a lab coat and stethoscope, but holding a pair of pliers and a wrench? Why couldn't a shop specializing in classical music tapes and CDs use a cartoonlike Beethoven character? Why couldn't a pet grooming shop use a cartoon of a primped pup?

Add Your Address and Phone Number

The name of your business and a graphic are, of course, the critical elements of a logo. But I strongly suggest that you consider including your address and phone number in your logo as well, for two reasons.

1. You'll make sure it is set in a type that is complementary to the main type in your logo and in a consistent format.

2. Even more important, you'll always know it's there. When you order a print ad, all you need to do is write "logo" in the position you want it. You will know that your address and phone number will automatically be included in the ad. If you rely on a printer to set your address and phone number each time you run an ad, you risk getting it in a typeface that doesn't fit well with your logo or having it left out altogether.

Should you include your hours of operation? This is optional. You certainly want them to appear in your print media ads, but hours can be cumbersome to work with in a logo. If your hours of operation are an important part of your marketing strategy (for instance, if you're pushing convenience), then include them in your logo.

Remember the Context

Finally, remember that in most cases your logo isn't going to appear on a stand-alone basis. It will be part of a context—a print or electronic media ad, your letterhead and envelopes, a sign in front of your building, your employees' uniforms, your delivery truck. Make sure that the finished logo will comfortably fit these various contexts.

For example, an extremely horizontal logo—say one that is three or four times wider than it is tall—might be hard to work with in a newspaper ad, especially a small space ad, or on a vertical brochure. In order to fit the logo into the width limitation, you might have to reduce it so much that it would become hard to read.

WHERE TO GET YOUR LOGO INEXPENSIVELY

Getting a unique logo for your business does not have to be complicated or even expensive. Although getting professional assistance is helpful (more about this in a minute), it isn't essential. You *can* put together a basic and serviceable logo for your business on a do-it-yourself basis. Here's how:

1. Go to any full-line print shop or typesetting service and ask for the type book. Ask the shop to let you take it home for a few days.

2. At first, flip through the book quickly, just to get a feel for all the different styles and approaches.

3. Then go through the book more slowly. If a type strikes your fancy for any reason, mark that page with a paper clip. I'll bet that you'll end up with dozens of pages marked, representing a wide variety of typefaces.

4. Narrow down your choices to three or four. This may be the toughest step. You have to do a real balancing act between making sure that your logo is distinctive and readable and having it somehow reflect the image you're trying to develop.

5. Once you've narrowed your type choices to not more than three or four, you can think about adding a graphic element. Many full-line printers and office supply shops and most art supply stores have what are called clip art books. These are literally hundreds of pages of drawings, cartoons, photographs, squiggles, lines, borders, and other shapes to choose from. They're called clip art because that's what you do: clip them out and integrate them into your logo.

6. Unless you have a flair for art or graphics, and most small business operators don't, I'd suggest that you do not try to actually design a finished logo yourself. Rather, take the three or four typefaces you like and the one or two graphic elements you like to your printer, explain that you're looking for a logo, and talk about why you like the different type styles and graphics and perhaps how you think the type and graphics might be integrated. Let the printer come up with a half dozen or so variations for you to look at. If you're lucky, you'll get a winner on the first round. More likely, you'll get one or two that are close to what you're after. In this case, have the printer revise and try again. Eventually, you'll get something you really like.

7. Once you've arrived at a logo you like, have the printer run off several dozen copies of it. Give them to all your ad reps, any printers you work with, any sign painters, and so on.

What I've just described is essentially a do-it-yourself approach. This approach will probably take the equivalent of a day of your time, stretched over two or three weeks, and shouldn't cost more than $150 to $200, unless you have the printer try a dozen logo variations and you go through three or four revisions.

If you don't want to spend the time involved in doing it yourself, or if you really feel the need for professional design assistance, you can work with a good desktop publisher or free-lance artist. Most of these folks charge by the hour ($25 to $50 an hour), so your cost is very much dependent on how much you have them do. However, you should be able to get a very good logo design from one of these sources for $500, or perhaps $750.

While at first blush this might seem like a lot, think about the variety of critical marketing functions the logo will perform and that you'll be using it for years and years.

Getting Started Tomorrow Morning

Start a collection of logos you like. It doesn't make any difference whether or not they are in your industry or whether they are for local or national companies. Look for them in magazines and newspapers and on brochures.

Think about why these particular logos strike your fancy. Is it the typeface? Is it the graphic element? Is it some unusual visual treatment? Is it the overall look or feel you get from the logo? Are there any patterns to the logos you like—are they all in a similar type style or do they all use a certain graphic approach?

8

Developing
Your Own Brochure

Yᵒᵘ may be a little surprised by this recommendation, because it is not one I have ever heard or seen elsewhere. I
believe that every business should have two pieces of marketing materials, no matter what. The first one you'll think
of right off the bat—it's the traditional business card. The second
one is a brochure. I cannot think of a single example of a business
that doesn't need some kind of basic brochure. Even a retail store
needs one.

Why do I place so much importance on a brochure? Because a
brochure is a logical extension of your business card. A business
card carries your logo, the name of your business, its address, its
phone numbers (including fax), perhaps its hours, and maybe a very
brief indication of what it does, such as a slogan. But that's about it.

This is where a brochure can pick up the ball and run with it.
A brochure expands on what your business is and what it does and,
most important, helps establish how it is different from (translate
that as better than) the competition.

You should hand out a brochure about as quickly as you hand
out a business card.

HOW ELABORATE SHOULD IT BE?

Does your brochure have to be an elaborate and expensive four-
color job, printed on stiff, slick stock? No, it doesn't. In fact, for most
small businesses, it should not be, if for no other reason than this:
As I said, you should be handing out your brochure almost as often
as you hand out a business card. If you are at all hesitant about

giving someone your fancy, four-color brochure that cost you an arm and a leg to print because you wonder if this prospect is worth the cost of the brochure, you've negated the very reason for having a brochure in the first place.

Brochures do you no good sitting in a drawer or on a shelf. This would be a little like spending a bundle on producing a spectacular MTV-like TV ad, then letting the tape sit in a drawer because you couldn't afford to put it on the air.

Certainly we could come up with all sorts of examples of businesses that probably need a fancy color brochure: championship golf resorts, upscale condominiums, and high-end investments. But the fact is, for most small businesses, a one- or two-color brochure with some monochrome photos or graphics will do quite nicely. And you won't second-guess yourself about handing it out in quantity.

USES OF BROCHURES

One of the great advantages of brochures is their flexibility. They can take on different formats to perform different roles. This, in turn, makes trying to categorize them a little tricky, since the dividing line between categories is often fuzzy at best. But, in the context of the small, hands-on business, nonprofit agency, or volunteer group for which this book is being written, we can basically say brochures fall into three broad categories: capabilities brochures, product brochures, and image or pride brochures.

Capabilities Brochures

These are, as the name suggests, your story as you want to tell it.

This type of brochure talks about your business as an organization. It talks about the origins of the business, who the principals and/or founders are, and why they founded the business. It should explore the business's goals and mission. It will certainly explain in some detail what your business does, with product or service listings and perhaps brief explanatory paragraphs. Most important of all, it will go to great pains to clearly demonstrate in what ways your business is different from its competition.

This is the kind of brochure I had in mind when I said that, after your business card, the next piece of marketing material any business owner should develop is a brochure.

Capabilities brochures are handed out to customers or potential customers at your place of business, at trade shows, at social or business meetings, and the like. They are used as leave-behind pieces when your sales representatives make calls. And they are the foundation for any kind of fund drive or membership drive by a nonprofit agency or a volunteer organization.

Product Brochures

Where a capabilities brochure is the umbrella that talks about the whole organization, product brochures focus on the specific products or services being offered. Depending on the type of organization you have, you could end up with a half dozen or more of these brochures.

Although there may be good reasons for you to develop your own product or service brochures, you should at least look into what kind of product or marketing brochures your manufacturers or suppliers might have available. These are often very slick, professional-looking brochures that you can buy from the manufacturer at a much lower per brochure cost than you could ever hope to print them for on your own. And generally there's space reserved for you to imprint your business's name, address, and phone number.

You'll normally find product or service brochures used in a sales context—which, of course, can include soliciting contributions or a new membership drive. Product or service brochures can be included in direct mail prospecting packets, be part of handout packets at a trade show, or be used by sales reps on personal calls, which, again, can include volunteers raising money for a charitable group.

Image or Pride Brochures

These are the fancy, four-color jobs printed on slick, heavy stock. For most small businesses, they can be reserved for really special occasions, like a significant anniversary or a major expansion.

TIPS ON DESIGNING AND WRITING A BASIC BROCHURE

Here are some tips to at least get you started developing a basic capabilities brochure for your business.

• For nine out of ten small businesses, you should develop your copy first, then add the visual elements or graphics to emphasize points in the copy. Why? Because, once again, the basic function of this type of brochure is to tell your story as you want it told.

Of course, there are many businesses for which the visual presentation might come first; a beauty shop comes to mind. The owner might want to have professional photographs taken to illustrate the shop's various services, then write copy to support the visual presentation.

But, for most small businesses, it will probably work the other way around. Develop the copy first—the history of the organization, its goals and mission, its products and services, its uniqueness in the marketplace. Then develop graphic elements to illustrate those points.

But, please, no pretty pictures—what the trade calls image art—that have little, if anything, to do with what is being presented. Oh, I know the justification: "It'll attract attention." Perhaps. But if you're going to include graphics in the first place, why stop at just attracting attention? Why not take the next step and find or develop graphics that also specifically reinforce what you're trying to get across in the copy?

• If you have an established visual style for your print media ads (for example, you always use a certain border or typeface or layout format), then design your brochure to reflect that style. If you are preparing the brochure before you have developed any print media ads, use a format for the brochure that will be easy to pick up in your ads.

• Your brochure copy should be written from the customer's point of view, not yours. That might seem as obvious as pointing out that the sun came up today. But you'd be surprised at how often brochure copy ends up being what the business owner wants to say, rather than what the customer wants to know.

Here are a couple of tricks for getting a customer viewpoint into your copy. Ask your salespeople, especially the front-line folks, to develop draft copy for the brochure. Or, better yet, ask a couple of your best customers to write the copy for you. You might be surprised at what you get.

• Eliminate as many decisions as you can. Your copy should always assume that the prospect will buy (or take a positive action). This means that you avoid qualifying words like "if" and "maybe," which assume the possibility of a negative response.

• Never ask open-ended questions. Always make sure that a question is phrased in such a way that the answer is a positive one— a yes instead of a no.

• Use action words and suggest that the reader take action— call us now, stop in and see us soon, return the enclosed postcard for more information today.

• As we've said before, always stress benefits to the reader, not the features of the products.

Lipstick might be available in dozens of colors, homogenized for smoothness, packaged in a handy, lightweight plastic tube that comes with a built-in mirror. These are the product's features. And who cares?

The benefits to the customer are that the colors are sensuous and will make your lips more attractive (presumably to men), that the homogenizing makes it easier to apply, and that the built-in mirror is very convenient to use.

• Avoid stiff phrasing and a formal tone. I've heard the excuse a hundred times: "But we want to sound professional." To most readers, "professional" equals "dull."

• Some tricks for structuring a brochure:

—Use wide margins and lots of white space. You do not want any pages that are gray with type.
—Print your copy ragged right, which means that the right-hand margin is *not* justified. Why? Because it's easier to read.
—Use not more than nine or ten lines of type per paragraph and not more than two or three sentences per paragraph. Insert a blank line between paragraphs.
—Capitalize the first word of a paragraph.

—Indent or underscore or use bold type to stress major benefits.

STRENGTHS AND WEAKNESSES OF BROCHURES

The strengths of brochures include the following:

• You have absolute control over what is said and how, including visual presentation.

• You have excellent audience selectivity; that is, you control almost completely who gets your brochure.

• Brochures are very flexible. There are lots of different formats that you can choose from for specialized purposes. They are also flexible in that there is lots of room for trade-offs—maybe you can skip using heavy-weight stock to print on so that you can afford to get an artist to do a custom sketch for you—while still retaining overall effectiveness.

• You can design and write a serviceable brochure yourself. There are also lots of affordable sources for help with the overall project or with specific parts you might be having trouble with, from desktop publishers to free-lance writers or artists.

Brochures have some weaknesses you need to be aware of as well:

• While you should never be reluctant to hand out your brochure to just about anyone who'll take it, ultimately a brochure has limited distribution potential. It is not a mass promotion vehicle and should never be thought of as a replacement for media promotion.

• If your situation does dictate a more elaborate brochure (four-color photographs on slick paper, for example), it can represent a significant out-of-pocket expense.

• The information in a brochure can become out of date.

Getting Started Tomorrow Morning

Go to your nearest chamber of commerce office, economic development agency, or tourism bureau. Stand back and look at all the brochures on display in the rack. For this purpose it doesn't make any difference if you're in the tourism/hospitality industry or not.

Which brochures do you want to pick up? Why? Was it because some visual trick caught your eye? Was it because a headline caught your attention? Was it because the topic was of particular interest to you?

Now, because it's said that we learn more from our failures than from our successes, actually take out the brochures that you did *not* look at originally. Give some thought to each of the following questions. Perhaps even take some notes:

- Why didn't you look at them?
- What was it, specifically, about each of these brochures that made you initially skip right over it?
- Was it the lack of an eye-catching graphic?
- Was it the use of a typeface that was hard to read?
- Was it that the headline didn't make sense or didn't have any sales appeal? Was the headline merely a label, rather than something that piqued your curiosity?
- Was it that because of the way the brochures are displayed on the rack, all of the important stuff (the headline, etc.) was literally hidden by other brochures?
- Was it because it was printed on a blah colored stock or because of a dull combination of stock and ink color?

9

How Your Business Looks

ANECDOTE 1: When I was a kid growing up in the suburbs of Chicago, I remember going to Riverview Amusement Park with my family. It was the Midwest's version of Coney Island. There were lots of rides and roller coasters. The ride I remember most was the parachute jump. You rode up to the top (it seemed like a hundred stories, but probably wasn't more than ten or twelve) in a seat for two. When you hit the top, a catch was released and you floated down on a parachute guided by wires at the corners. The view from the top was really spectacular, and your stomach did a wonderful little flip-flop between the time when the catch released and the point when the parachute filled with air.

Unfortunately, the other thing I remember most about Riverview was how dirty it was. Cigarette butts, soda cups (this was before the days of soda in cans), gum wrappers, hot dog papers, and who knows what else were heaped in windrows along the walkways and up against the fences. The sidewalks were literally sticky with spilled soda and gum. And most of the benches and buildings looked as if they hadn't been painted in years.

When Riverview closed, I remember reading an article speculating that the age of the amusement park was over, that television and hi-fi, both of which were just coming into their own, meant that people were going to stay home more. As I recall, the article even hinted that other forms of outdoor entertainment, such as big league baseball and professional football, were in danger of succumbing to the electronic revolution. But that's another story.

Of course, in hindsight we can see the phenomenal success of the theme parks created by Disney, Six Flags, and others that replaced the defunct Riverviews and Coney Islands.

Today's theme park is a significant step up from the old amusement park. The rides are far more hair-raising. The developers understand the importance of constantly adding new, even more thrilling rides to give people a reason to come back. And there are costumed Mickey and Minnie Mouse or Bugs Bunny and Tweety Bird characters running around to add a sense of fun and excitement.

But, in the success of today's theme park, an almost obsessive emphasis on maintaining the park's first-class physical appearance is nearly as important as the "spectacularness." Now, if you drop a cigarette butt or toss away a gum wrapper, within seconds a uniformed kid with a broom and pan will whisk it away. Now, instead of windrows of trash lining the walkways, there are raised flower beds filled with geraniums, marigolds, and snapdragons. Now, there are banners and colorful hangings everywhere, and the buildings and benches are freshly painted.

Was the fact that it had become so grungy the reason Riverview closed? It probably wasn't the only reason. But you'll never convince me that it was not one of several reasons.

ANECDOTE 2: Some twenty-five years ago we had the occasion to visit Vancouver, British Columbia. In one sense calling it a visit is an overstatement. We were on our way to Alaska and spent perhaps all of an hour and a half driving through Vancouver to get to the docks where we would board the car ferry that would carry us north.

It was mid-June, and I have one outstanding memory of that visit: There were flowers everywhere. Every public and commercial building had beautifully manicured and highly visible flower beds. Virtually every home sported some kind of flower display, ranging from large and colorful beds to just a pot of geraniums on a front stoop.

There could have been bums lying in the gutter and heaps of litter and trash on the street corners. The buildings may have been dilapidated and run-down. But, if that was the case, I sure didn't see it. All I saw was that glorious and continuous array of colorful flowers.

ANECDOTE 3: Our local electrical contracting company has a dozen or more trucks of one kind or another. All are a bright, fire-engine red. And all are washed regularly.

Of course, they all have the company's name prominently displayed on their sides. But even when you can't see the company name, the bright red color and shiny cleanliness are highly visible and easily recognized.

Has the company's commitment to keeping its trucks bright and clean meant more business? Without an in-depth market recognition survey, there's probably no way to tell. But I do know that I see a lot of those trucks around the community.

ANECDOTE 4: There are several pancake house restaurants in our area that are part of a chain. They've been present in the community for at least fifteen years. Over those fifteen years I can think of at least four times that the restaurants have been completely redecorated.

They usually close for a week. The carpeting is torn up and replaced with new. The upholstery on the booths is replaced. The light fixtures are replaced. All the interior walls are repapered or repainted. And the exterior trim and roof are repainted. In other words, about every three or four years, the restaurants "renew" themselves.

TOTAL AMBIENCE

This, of course, brings me to the point of this chapter: The total ambience of your business is a key factor in your overall marketing strategy. I'm not just talking about a dab of paint and some potted flowers, although they are important. Rather, I'm talking about the total look and feel that you present to your customers and potential customers and the "message" that it sends.

I suppose it's conceivable to imagine some kind of business where the seller and the buyer never meet, perhaps only communicating by phone, fax, or computer modem. In that case, if the seller operates from a filthy and paper-littered office and sits around, unwashed and unshaven, in worn-out jeans and a torn T-shirt, it doesn't make any difference. But I would suggest to you that this is the rare exception.

Most of the rest of us operate more or less in a fishbowl. We have a building and surrounding land that can be seen by passersby. We have an office or shop to which customers come. We have parking areas. We have merchandise displays. We have things hung on the wall. We play music over a sound system or over the telephone while callers are on hold. We have people who interact face-to-face with customers or clients. We have trucks and other equipment that go out into the marketplace to deliver, make service calls, or do other kinds of work.

These are all part of the image our business presents to our customers and potential customers. They are as much a part of how we promote our business as our paid ads, brochures, and special events. You underestimate their importance at grave risk.

LET YOUR CUSTOMERS DECIDE

Who decides what the image of your business should be? There's no question that it needs to be your customers and potential customers.

Remember the anecdote in my introduction about how, when I'm looking for traditional men's wear, if I walk into a shop that's playing rock music, I turn around and walk out because I assume the shop doesn't have anything I would be interested in? My suspicion is that in most cases the rock music is being played over the store's sound system because that's what the young people who work there like to listen to. But what if the majority of your customers and potential customers don't, in fact, like rock music?

It should be the likes and dislikes of your customers, not your own personal whims or the whims of your staff, that are the governing factor in choosing the elements of how you present your business.

The true entrepreneur is probably bristling at that statement. Having the independence to do it your way, to make your own decisions, to be who you want to be rather than who somebody else wants you to be, is probably the single most prevalent reason most people start their own businesses. So now I come along saying that you have to kowtow to the personal whims of your customers.

Am I really suggesting that you should try to be someone you're not? For instance, that you and your staff should all be wearing business suits to impress your customers, even though you are not comfortable in business suits? Hardly.

Rather, what I'm suggesting is that if you are not a business suit–type person, perhaps you should not consider going into a busi-

clothing store's sound system. Besides music on the sound system, what other sounds might your customers hear? What will you play on the phone system when people are on hold? Some businesses, like print shops and auto repair centers, are obviously going to be noisy. But what about the less than obvious sources of sound? What about telephones, copiers, and other office machines? Heating and air conditioning or other types of equipment? What about the need for your people to talk to one another? Or exterior noise, such as traffic on a busy street or from a neighboring business?

Give some thought to the sound ambience of your business. Are there potential sources of sounds that could be offensive to your customers?

Finally, how will your business feel to customers, literally? This obviously includes heating and/or cooling, but "feel" goes beyond just maintaining a comfortable temperature. Feel has to do with what's under a customer's feet, carpeting or concrete. Feel has to do with what customers can touch with their hands: countertops and displays. Feel has to do with what customers might sit on in a waiting area or while talking to one of your customer service reps.

Although the feel of a business is probably not of crucial importance to its success or failure, it nonetheless deserves at least some thought just to make sure there isn't some aspect that will turn out to be potentially offensive to your customers.

Getting Started Tomorrow Morning

Most of us respond unconsciously to the total ambience created by a business's visual, auditory, olfactory, and tactile aspects. When we enter a place for the first time, our senses gather a quick first impression. We consciously notice only elements that are either very negative or very positive. The point of this exercise is to raise your conscious awareness of how sight, sound, smell, and touch can help shape your feelings about a business.

On a legal pad, write down the names of the places where you do the majority of your food shopping, personal clothing shopping, banking, and eating out. Now close your eyes and answer the following questions about each one of the four (jot down notes if you like):

- What are the very first things you see when you walk through the door? What objects? What colors? What hangings on the wall? What people? What are they wearing? What are their facial expressions, their body demeanor?
- What do you first hear when you enter? Are they sounds that you would normally associate with that business? Do you hear music? What kind of music?
- What do you immediately smell when you enter? Is it a smell you would expect with this kind of business?
- What is the first thing you feel? Is it the temperature—too warm or too cold? Is it the floor covering?

Now, think of three or four businesses you have been to, but do not like to go to. These can be any businesses. Answer the same questions about each:

- What was the first thing you saw when you entered?
- What was the first thing you heard?
- What did you smell?
- What did you feel?

Here's the tough part of the exercise. Try to analyze to what degree each aspect of the business's sensory ambience had an influence on your decision to do business there or not to do business there. Certainly aspects like price, selection, service, and convenience of location will probably be the major influences on your decision to select one business over another. But can you honestly say that how a business looks, sounds, smells, and feels had absolutely no effect whatsoever?

10

Your Personal Sales Staff

T he people on your staff who have personal contact with customers—the behind the counter staff, the door-to-door crew, the telemarketing bunch, and the "road warriors"—for some reason are usually not thought of as being part of your marketing effort. Yet, your personal sales effort is without a doubt one of the most important elements in your overall marketing program.

The fact is, there are very few businesses that do not require some kind of personal interaction between staff and customers. And this doesn't just mean the people who are directly responsible for sales. It also means the installation and service people, secretaries and receptionists, clerical staff, and even security guards, to mention just a few. In other words, anyone who has contact with customers is in some way directly or indirectly "selling" the organization.

ONLY PEOPLE CAN SELL

Think about it for a moment. Paid advertising or positive publicity in the media, a big once-a-year clearance sale, even a heavily promoted special event can at best only get bodies through the door. It takes personal salespeople to close the sale. Only living, breathing human beings can:

• Establish an immediate, one-on-one relationship with a customer. They can smile, greet the customer, engage the customer in a conversation, and put him or her at ease. They can create the brief, but all-important feeling of trust that is the basic requirement before the customer will make a positive buy decision.

• Learn a customer's specific needs. By listening carefully, by gentle but persistent inquiry, by seeking confirmation and clarification, and sometimes by a little imaginative reading between the lines, they can figure out what a customer is really looking for.

• Adapt a sales pitch to respond to a customer's specific needs or real wants. In other words, they are flexible. They can focus on and stress the aspects of a product or service that address what the customer is looking for.

• Emphasize how the product or service is unique in the marketplace and in what specific ways it is superior to its competition.

• Solve problems. Of all of the things that live salespeople can do, this is one of the most important.

Again, think about it for a moment. A sale is rarely just a sale. Most of the time, when a customer walks through the door, or telephones, he or she has some kind of problem.

Maybe the customer sees the problem as starting with you—an order got goofed up, billing was incorrect, or something you sold him doesn't work properly. Or maybe he or she sees the problem as being his or hers—something has worn out and she needs a replacement; he's looking for some expert outside help to accomplish a goal; her company has grown and she thinks there's a need for more equipment, but she isn't sure which models best suit her needs.

In any case, what customers want from the first person they see or talk to is a solution to their problem. Or, if not a solution, at least some empathy—an acknowledgment that they do, indeed, have a problem—and a sincere effort to get them the help they want.

• Finally, ask for the order! "We'd like to have your business"; "I'll write this order up right away"; "Let's open an account for you now."

THE INS AND OUTS

Traditionally there are two major categories of people who are directly involved in sales:

1. *Inside Sales.* These folks interact with customers from inside your place of business; that is, customers come to them. They include the folks who work the floor, those who stand behind the counter, and those who take orders over the phone from existing customers.

2. *Outside Sales.* These people work with customers outside of your place of business; in other words, they go to the customers. They include people who sell door-to-door, people who conduct home parties, route drivers, and, of course, the traditional traveling salespeople, whether they just drive around town or jet all over the country.

However, as products and services have become more and more technical and/or more and more complicated, sales has increasingly become a team effort rather than strictly a solo job. Here are some of the new categories of salespeople:

• *Telemarketers.* This category is differentiated from inside salespeople for two reasons: First, because so many businesses are now making regular use of telemarketing, and second, because telemarketers are essentially electronic canvassers, generally looking for new customers and/or qualified leads rather than focusing on servicing existing customers, as inside salespeople tend to do.

• *Account Representatives or Account Executives.* These folks are more or less analogous to the old outside salesperson. They make calls on potential new customers. They do an initial assessment of the customer's needs and wants, then call in one or more technical specialists to actually determine which of the company's products or services will best meet the customer's needs and how.

• *Sales Engineers or Technical Specialists.* The job of these members of the sales team isn't to make initial calls, but to work with the customer's technical people after a relationship has been established to make sure your products or services meet the customer's specific needs.

• *Customer Service Representatives.* CSRs, as they're often called, are usually inside people who have a strong clerical background, but are also very good at customer service. In effect, their job is to take over after a front-line salesperson has submitted the order. They do the follow-up, making sure the order gets through the system on time and correctly, answering any questions, and solving any problems that might pop up.

EXPECTATIONS AND COMPENSATION

One of the more common problems I find with owners of small businesses, especially those who have no background in sales or marketing, is that they have completely unrealistic expectations of what salespeople can accomplish.

For example, I am regularly asked by the owner of a new business if I will help him or her find somebody willing to do sales calls for commission only. In other words, the owner expects the sales rep to be self-supporting from day one.

What the business owner soon learns is that no experienced salesperson will be the least bit interested in this proposition, and that anyone who is interested (which usually means a sales beginner) either doesn't work out (i.e., doesn't produce the expected/necessary results) or quits after a short time because he or she can't make a living working on commission only.

The fact is, commission-based sales compensation programs work well only for established businesses that have lots of marketplace recognition and an established customer base. The sales rep is able to more or less easily gain entry to the people who make buying decisions and doesn't have to spend a great deal of time establishing credibility. In other words, the sales rep can get to the order stage (i.e., the commission-producing stage) in a relatively short time.

On the other hand, most new businesses and/or new products in the marketplace tend to require a lot of what are called "pioneering" sales, which means that before an actual sale can be made, the sales rep must devote a good deal of time and effort to creating product awareness and establishing how the product meets a customer's needs—perhaps a need the customer doesn't even know he or she has!

In other words, for most new businesses or new products, orders (i.e., commission-generating sales) are few and far between, at least in the introductory stages. This is why the sales compensation program needs to be salary-based rather than commission only.

TWO KINDS OF SALESPEOPLE

There are two kinds of outside salespeople, order takers and order getters.

Order takers are very good at servicing existing customers. Their sales approach tends to be more service-oriented, with a strong emphasis on maintaining good customer relations. Their personalities tend to be sociable, accommodating, outgoing, and patient.

On the other hand, order getters are very good at ferreting out and closing new customers. They are not afraid to meet strangers and are undaunted by turn-downs. In fact, the best order getters do not recognize the word "no"; to them a "no" is nothing but a challenge to find a way to turn it into a "yes." Their sales approach tends to be much more assertive. Their personalities tend to the aggressive and goal-oriented.

Which kind you hire depends on how you are going to use the salesperson. Order getters are not always better than order takers. In fact, in some sales contexts an order getter's aggressiveness might actually be a detriment.

Hire an order taker if your business fits two or more of the following:

- It has been in business in your defined marketplace for at least three years.
- It has an established and stable customer base.
- Its products and/or services are familiar in the marketplace.
- Its products and/or services do not undergo volatile changes from year to year (i.e., shifting fashion trends, new generations of high tech).
- Its competitors are known to it and are not making aggressive moves against it.

Hire an order getter if your business qualifies under two or more of the following:

- It is a new business trying to enter the marketplace.
- It has a new product that you are trying to introduce into the marketplace.
- Its existing customer base is eroding for any reason and you need to generate new replacement customers.
- The existing competition has become much more aggressive, especially targeting your customer group.
- A new competitor has entered the marketplace.

HOW SALESPEOPLE MOTIVATE THEMSELVES

The business book section of your favorite bookstore or library is filled with books on how to motivate salespeople. There always seems to be somebody offering a motivational workshop or seminar for salespeople. The subject of how to motivate salespeople to top performance really demands much more space than this volume can possibly give it.

However, based on my experience in hiring and supervising dozens of salespeople over the years, there is one bit of insight on sales motivation I want to share with you, if for no other reason than to save you the frustration I felt until I figured it out.

Every successful salesperson develops an individual technique for getting up to hit the street. However, in my experience, salespeople mostly fall into two broad categories. I call them the sandbaggers and the shoot-for-the-mooners.

To illustrate, let's say 1,000 of something is a realistic goal—it can be 1,000 units, $1,000 per week in new orders, whatever. Given the goal of 1,000, the sandbagger's first reaction will be to say, "No way we can make that. The moon is in the wrong phase. The economy is going to pot. Our biggest customer just had a layoff. The best we can do is 600; if we're lucky, maybe 700!" Then the sandbagger will hit the street and come back with 1,002, shaking his or her head and muttering, "I don't believe it."

Meanwhile, given the goal of 1,000, the shoot-for-the-mooner will scoff, "Only a thousand. Heck, we're gonna blitz that market-place. They'll never know what hit 'em. We can do 1,300, no sweat!" And the shoot-for-the-mooner will hit the street and come back with 1,002, shaking his or her head and muttering, "I tried everything I knew."

What you need to understand is that neither one is in any way consciously trying to deceive you. Each is using his or her own natural motivation system. Sandbaggers always have to exceed their goals; they get up by building on success. Shoot-for-the-mooners, on the other hand, always have to reach further than they can grasp; they get up by stretching themselves.

There is nothing wrong with being a sandbagger or with being a shoot-for-the-mooner. The only thing wrong is if you are a sales-person and don't know which type you are, or if you are a sales supervisor and don't understand the type you're dealing with and, therefore, try to make them into something they're not.

WHAT TO LOOK FOR IN A SALES REP

Here's a quick overview of the characteristics I learned to look for when I was hiring salespeople. These are roughly in the order of priority I looked for them—more on this later:

• A genuine interest in people. Salespeople have to deal with all kinds of different folks in all kinds of different situations. A success-ful salesperson has to have a strong undercurrent of sociability, has to like people. Misanthropes have no business in sales.

• A natural enthusiasm. It's been my experience that in the real world of sales, a sales rep's enthusiasm can be a major factor in a customer's decision to say yes. How many times have you been turned off by a sales rep who didn't seem to care about you or about what he or she was selling?

• Sincerity. This goes hand in hand with enthusiasm and liking people. Salespeople who come across as sincere in their efforts have taken a giant step toward establishing that all-important, albeit brief, relationship of trust that is necessary before a customer will say yes.

• Experience and/or training. The first kind of experience or training I looked for was anything that involved good customer service skills. It scored lots of points with me if a candidate for a sales job had taken one or more workshops or classes in customer service skills. It also scored points if he or she had "just" volunteered for years as a museum tour guide (i.e., been involved with people).

• Finally, I looked for experience and/or training in the specific product or service area that the salesperson would be selling.

I can see the eyebrows going up. Why wouldn't experience and training in the product or service be at the very top of my list?

Because what I found is that in most sales fields, particularly in retail sales, so-called soft factors like enthusiasm, sincerity, and listening to what the customer is really asking for had as much to do with a positive buy decision as price or quality or extensive product knowledge. In most fields, the specifics of the product or service can be learned relatively easily. What cannot be taught are basic personality traits, such as liking people and sincerely wanting to help them.

Getting Started Tomorrow Morning

Think about the things you've bought in the last month or so. Certainly this will include many routine, everyday purchases, like groceries, a meal at a restaurant, socks, a hardware item, or office supplies. But it might also include more substantial items, such as a new suit or dress, insurance, a major appliance or piece of furniture, a computer, or a vehicle. Write down on a piece of legal paper at least five examples of routine purchases and two or three examples of unusual or major purchases.

Now try to recall the individual salespeople who were involved in those different purchases. Can you remember any of them specifically? Why or why not? Were any of them outstanding, either positively or negatively, for any reason? Can you honestly say that a sales representative's personality had no impact whatsoever on your decision to buy a particular item or had no influence on where you bought that item?

11

The Importance of Good Customer Service

ANECDOTE 1: I live in a medium-size urban area (about 375,000). I moved here in the mid-1960s. Not long after I moved into my house, a neighbor told me that if I ever needed hardware items, *the* place to go was K&K Hardware.

In itself, this was no big thing. Lots of folks have favorite places they like to recommend to others (see Chapter 12, "Word-Of-Mouth Promotion"). However, what *was* remarkable about this particular recommendation was that K&K was on the opposite side of the urban area. It was easily a twenty-five-minute drive away, and to get there you literally had to pass by or near at least a half dozen other hardware stores.

Why did this hardware store rate such a singular recommendation? Because no matter which salesperson you met when you walked in the door, he or she was able to quickly take you to the right shelf to find the exact product you needed to solve your hardware problem.

K&K's people knew their products and knew their store—all of it. However, what they also very clearly understood was that most people who walked through the door did *not* know what specific item they were looking for. Rather, they had a problem and were looking for a solution.

In fact, K&K Hardware is so widely known in the community that everyone seems to have a favorite story about how it solved some unusual problem. One friend's is how K&K was able to sell him a peavey handle from stock. A peavey is one of those lumberman's tools with a long spike and hinged hook on one end that is used to push logs around in the water. A peavey might be a common in-stock item in the north woods, but it certainly isn't often asked for in the heart of Midwestern corn country.

From a marketing standpoint, K&K's accomplishment is incredible. Based on a strategy of total customer service, it has achieved almost complete domination of the marketplace, if not necessarily in terms of revenue, certainly in terms of reputation and name recognition. Now remember, I'm talking about the mid-1960s, long before Tom Peters articulated the crucial importance of quality customer service in *In Search of Excellence*.

ANECDOTE 2: I recently read that many companies that had gone to one of those automated phone answering systems, so-called voice mail (you know, the kind that tells you to punch in the extension of your party if known or punch in zero to talk to a live body), were abandoning them because of customer anger.

These companies are discovering that the amount of money they might save by eliminating or reducing the expense of a live phone operator was more than offset by the lost business from frustrated customers or potential customers who simply hung up on the machine.

ANECDOTE 3: I enjoy music, especially jazz. I am old enough to remember a time when if you found a record by a new artist and weren't sure you would like it, you could go into a little room and listen to some or all of it before you bought it. More than once I have passed up an album (now CD) because I didn't have the opportunity to listen to it first.

Recently my wife and I dropped into a local music retailer called Coop Records. We were leafing through the jazz CDs and had partially lifted out one by Alex Bugnon, an acoustic pianist, when one of the salespeople approached. He noticed the album and asked, "Have you heard him before?" We said that no, we hadn't. He immediately took the CD, opened it, and started playing it on the store's stereo system.

While listening to the music, we continued to chat and commented that we liked Kenny G, David Sanborn, and other sax artists. He then went to the CD bin, pulled out another album, and said, "If you like Kenny G, you'll like this guy." It was George Howard. He fired it up on the store's stereo.

We walked out having purchased both CDs.

ANECDOTE 4: A friend of mine owns and operates an independent pharmacy. He once told me that he can buy aspirin off the shelf at one of the major national discount chains at a lower price than he can buy it from his own supplier because the discounter buys it by the truckload and he only buys it by the case.

However, as part of his business, he also has a home medical supply service, supplying wheelchairs, hospital beds, oxygen, walkers, commodes—whatever is needed. Each one of his people, including the kid who drives the delivery truck, is thoroughly trained in the assembly and use of the equipment.

ANECDOTE 5: There is a department store in our community called Von Maur's. It's part of a small Midwestern regional chain. But it has gotten the word! When you enter the store, you hear quiet piano music played by a live person on a baby grand. Nearby are comfortable chairs and lots of magazines. The chairs are more often than not occupied by men, relaxing while their wives are shopping. When you buy something at the store and pay for it by check or credit card (i.e., when you give them an address), within a week you'll get a nice handwritten, signed postcard of thanks from the salesperson.

THE SMALL-BUSINESS COMPETITIVE EDGE

It's called customer service. And it had better be as integral a part of the day-to-day operation of your business as breathing is a routine part of your day-to-day living. Indeed, the one is as critical to your survival as a business as the other is to your survival as a living human being.

In fact, customer service may be *the* single most important competitive weapon small business has against the big boys. Some have even suggested that it is the only one!

My anecdote about the pharmacist illustrates two points:

1. Small businesses simply cannot effectively compete with the big boys on price or selection. A large company's sheer size (i.e., purchasing power) is one of its major strengths. A small business trying to compete head-to-head with one of the big boys on price or selection is like a welterweight getting into the ring with a heavyweight.

2. However, there are things the big boys cannot seem to do very effectively, and one of them is deliver good customer service.

Their staff members tend to be more stock clerks than sales representatives. They simply have too many different items and too few
people.

How many times have you been in one of the big chain merchandisers and looked all over the place for someone to help you,
only to have the person you find tell you that he or she doesn't work
in that department?

THE CUSTOMER AS THE CENTER OF THE UNIVERSE

Truly outstanding customer service means that everything you do—
and I mean that literally: *everything!*—revolves around anticipating
and meeting your customers' needs. Not yours, the customers'.
Period.

- The days and hours your business is open, where you and
  your staff and your service vehicles park (*not* right in front of
  your business), your location, the physical layout of your
  business
- The quality of the people you hire to staff your business and
  when you have them work, the emphasis you place on friendliness and sincerity in dealing with customers, how you train
  your staff
- The turnaround time on orders, the design of your order and
  other forms, your credit policies
- How many incoming phone lines you have, how many rings
  there are before a phone gets answered, what the person says
  when he or she picks up the phone, what customers hear if
  they are put on hold, how you handle it when people are out,
  including how quickly they return messages
- How flexible you allow your people to be to "bend the rules"
  to accommodate a customer
- How quickly your service people show up after a call, how
  precisely you can guarantee their arrival time, and how well
  equipped they are in terms of both training and on-board
  parts and tools to get the job done

- Whether you give free delivery and setup, offer free gift wrap, or carry house charge accounts
- Whether you offer your customers refreshments—a cup of coffee, soda, or a cookie

Truly outstanding customer service is not a selective policy (customers come first, but only under certain circumstances). Truly outstanding customer service is a way of life. It's an integral part of the way you do business.

Businesses can operate for their customers' convenience or for their own convenience. Businesses can survive or not survive. Is there a direct cause-and-effect relationship between businesses that have good customer service and those that survive and between those that do not have good customer service and those that do not survive? I'd suggest to you that the evidence is mounting that indeed there is.

Getting Started Tomorrow Morning

I must admit that I included this chapter only after some hesitation. My first reaction was not to say anything about customer service because I felt it was one of those "can of worms" topics that once opened had to be dealt with in a depth and breadth that was beyond the scope of this book. Ultimately, however, I opted to include this brief chapter because the topic of quality customer service is so important that it had to be at least acknowledged.

How does one get started on the path of good customer service? With a small first step.

If yours is an established business, you might start by asking your staff, especially your sales staff, if there is anything about your operation that "bugs" customers.

Of course, as good employees, their first instinct will be to tell you what you want to hear, which is, "nothing." Don't believe them; there is something. Maybe it's something big, maybe it's something small. But there are things that "bug" your customers, and your staff knows what they are.

Be persistent. Promise them that there will be no retribution. Give them the opportunity to reply in confidence. I guarantee that the longer you've been in business, the more of those "little things" that are there more for your convenience than for your customers' will have snuck into your operation. Find out what they are and get to work changing them.

If you're still in the planning stage, you have the chance to really do things right. As you design your operation, weigh every decision against this two-pronged question: How will this affect my customers, and will they perceive it as a positive or a negative?

12

Word-of-Mouth Promotion

I once was involved in the startup planning for a monthly magazine targeted at a mature audience. We did extensive prelaunch surveys to find out what the audience wanted to read. Travel (places to go and things to do) was very high on their interest list. As part of our surveying, we also asked what sources of information people relied on if they were interested in going to a certain place.

The number one source of information, by far, was friends, relatives, and neighbors—that is, people they knew. They would ask, "Have you been to so-and-so? How was it?"

A distant second was a trusted publication, such as a familiar newspaper or magazine. Paid media advertising was an even more distant third.

Of course, our surveys only confirmed what anyone in the hospitality and tourism industry already knew, that word of mouth was clearly the most powerful promotional medium.

My suggestion to you is that the tourism and hospitality industry is not unique in this. Word-of-mouth promotion can be the best friend or the worst enemy of just about any product or service being offered in the marketplace.

In fact, I would even go so far as to suggest that no amount of rah-rah paid promotion, no matter how well done or how strategically placed in the media, will be able to offset negative word of mouth if it's working against you.

This is particularly true for small businesses that have to live or die in relatively small, local markets. A marketer on a national scale can, at least for a time, hide behind the geographic diversity of the marketplace. On the other hand, the fact that many members of a local marketer's target group—and for our purposes this includes a business that is selling regionally or nationally, but to a well-defined niche—are in more or less regular contact means that word of mouth takes on a real sense of immediacy.

MOST POWERFUL, LEAST CONTROLLABLE

The irony about word-of-mouth promotion is that while it is the most powerful promotional medium of all, it is also the promotional technique over which the individual marketer has the least direct control. You can design your own television or newspaper ads. You can write and send out your own news releases. You can develop your own brochures and direct mail campaigns. But you can't directly control what people say about your business to their family, friends, or colleagues.

What's more, study after study has shown that an unhappy customer is far more likely to voluntarily share a bad experience—"Have you been to that new restaurant yet? Forget it. The food is terrible and the service is lousy!"—than a satisfied customer is to spread a good word—"Gee, we really had a great meal at that new restaurant!" In fact, studies say it is up to ten times more likely!

This is only human nature. Just think about how you tend to share your own experiences. If you've received poor customer service, you can hardly contain yourself, and you voluntarily share your story with all sorts of folks—"Boy, whatever you do, don't go to that new place over on Main Street. They were downright nasty when I tried to take something back that didn't fit." Yet if you really like a place, you tend to take it for granted and to share your feelings only if you're specifically asked—"Oh, yeah, I go there all the time. They really treat you great. In fact, there was this time that they went out of their way to solve a problem I had."

So, if a marketer can't exert much direct control over word-of-mouth promotion, should you just throw up your hands and let the marketplace have its say? Of course not. While there may not be much you can do to directly control what's said about your business through word of mouth, there are lots of things you can do to indirectly influence it.

Deliver What You Promise

There's no question that the number one thing you can do to head off negative word of mouth is simply to deliver what you promise. Don't play games with the marketplace. Lincoln's famous statement that "you can fool some of the people some of the time, but you can't fool all of the people all of the time" is as apt in marketing as it was for politics.

If you're positioning your business as the lowest-price place, make sure it is, indeed, the lowest-price place. Don't play the game of starting with inflated prices and marking them down with phony huge discounts so that they just appear to be low. My mother can walk through a supermarket and quote from memory both the "regular" price and the "special" price of dozens and dozens of items, not only at that supermarket, but at its competitors as well. Nobody fools her with phony discounts.

If you're going after the most convenient niche, be open twenty-four hours a day (or at least eighteen) and on Sunday.

If you're trying for an image as the friendliest, at least make sure your staff aren't all standing in a corner gossiping about their latest date or the results of the baseball playoffs. There are few things that make me as mad as being ignored when I'm looking for help.

However, in today's highly competitive marketplace, just heading off negative word of mouth won't be enough to differentiate your business from the competition, especially if yours is a new business. You need to take it a step further.

The number one thing you *can* do to promote positive word of mouth about your business is to deliver *more* than you promise—consistently.

If you're positioning your business as the lowest-price place, then not only do you make sure it really has the lowest prices, you let the customers know it does, graphically, by posting item-by-item price comparisons with your competitors.

If you're going after the most convenient niche, then not only is your business open twenty-four hours a day, seven days a week, but you throw in free pickup and delivery.

If you're trying for an image as the friendliest, then not only is your staff available, but they go out of their way to learn their customers' names, what color they prefer, and what size they wear.

Have a Clear Image

If delivering what you promise and more is one cornerstone of positive word-of-mouth promotion of your business, then having a clear image of what your business is is a second and virtually equally important one. We've said this before in various contexts, but it's worth reinforcing here, once again.

If yours is an existing business, what is it to its customers? If yours is a new business, what do you want it to be to its customers? If you recall, in Chapter 5, "Establishing Your Uniqueness," we said that most businesses can be only one thing to their customers or potential customers.

Being able to convey what that one thing is, simply and clearly, will greatly facilitate positive word-of-mouth promotion. If your customers and potential customers have a clear image of your business, if you have a memorable, descriptive name for your business, if you have a unique logo, consistently used, and if you continuously reinforce these through your promotions and advertising, then your customers can certainly more easily share them with other people.

On the other hand, if customers are confused or unclear as to what your business is, then, in effect, it is nothing to them, which means they are going to be much less likely to talk about it with others.

Ask Your Customers to Spread the Word

To encourage positive word-of-mouth promotion, your existing happy customers should be your best ally in spreading the word.

There are lots of small, subtle ways to use your present paid promotions to encourage positive word of mouth. In your print media ads, regularly use a tagline that suggests that customers tell a friend about your business. In your electronic ads, you might consider writing the ad as if it were a conversation between two friends. In your newsletters, include anecdotes about how regular customers refer friends to your business.

In fact, you can use real people in your ads and promotions, giving positive testimonials about your business. Regularly issue product bulletins with complimentary letters or testimonials from satisfied customers. Seeing a familiar, believable face on TV or in the newspaper saying something positive about your business or products will very much encourage people to pass the word along.

You can even design special promotions specifically to encourage your current customers to bring in new people. For example, you can host a by-invitation wine and cheese party with some special attraction—a designer trunk showing, a visiting VIP—where the price of admission for a regular customer is bringing a friend. Or, you can reward your existing customers by offering them a gift certificate if a new customer mentions that an existing customer referred them.

Do Something Outrageous

Word-of-mouth promotion does not necessarily have to be just positive testimonials. It can be any positive mention of your name.

So, to encourage people to talk about you, do something "outrageous." We cover this topic more thoroughly in Chapter 16, but it's worth touching on here in the context of word-of-mouth promotion.

Of course, *outrageous* is a highly relative term. Something that drives one man completely bonkers is another man's just good fun. The key to successfully pulling off being outrageous is for *you* to be comfortable with what you're doing. If you and your people are having fun with whatever you're planning, then the chances are it will come off that way to your customers. Here are a couple of ideas for being outrageous.

If yours is a new business and your strategy is to have the lowest prices in town, then for your grand opening give it away, literally. For example, instead of having a drawing with a single prize winner getting a trip or a product worth $2,000, say that the first twenty customers to show up on a certain day and time will each get a free $100 shopping spree.

If yours is an existing business and you want it to be known as the friendliest place, then rent a live elephant, hang a banner on it that says you're big on friendliness, and have your staff ride it through town. Of course, advertise that you're going to do it. You might even be surprised and end up with some news coverage as well.

DEALING WITH NEGATIVE WORD OF MOUTH

Unfortunately, negative word of mouth can get started all too easily and all too innocently.

Before we get into this, though, a reminder: No amount of positive paid promotions can offset negative word of mouth that is justified or deserved. If you've cut your service staff, no rah-rah campaign cynically claiming "we're big on service" is going to overcome angry and unhappy customers telling other people, "I have to call four or five times before I can get someone out to look at my machine!"

What I'm talking about here are the kinds of small, unintentional things that happen to a business that can inadvertently lead to negative word of mouth. One of your employees might be having personal problems and ends up by taking it out on the customers, perhaps just with discourteous service, or worse, by cheating them in some way. Or you may intentionally let your stock dwindle because you're planning to add a completely new line, but suddenly the rumor gets started that you're going out of business.

What do you do if you become aware that there is negative word of mouth spreading about your business? There is only one answer: You attack it quickly, and you attack it head-on. The worst thing you can do is to ignore negative word of mouth, hoping it will go away. There are a couple of reasons for this.

1. The longer it goes on, the more people will believe it ("Well, if it wasn't true, they'd have said so."). Don't worry that if you acknowledge negative word of mouth, you'll be reinforcing it. Your silence gives it far more credibility than getting it out in the open.

2. The longer it goes on, the harder it is to reach everyone who has heard the negative side with your positive side. The power of negative word of mouth grows exponentially: One person tells two others, now three people know; each of these tells two others, now seven people know; each of these tells two others, now fifteen people know, and so on.

Your best strategy by far is to do everything you can to turn the negative into a positive. If you know of specific customers who were treated badly by a disgruntled employee, send them a personal letter of apology. Better yet, make a personal call to explain that what happened to them was contrary to your way of doing business, then follow up with a letter of apology. If they were cheated or short-changed in some way, make restitution.

If a rumor gets started that you're going out of business, attack it head-on. Send a letter to all your customers saying that you're aware of the rumor and that it isn't true. Run "We're here to stay" ads. If yours is a prominent business, you might even want to hold a news conference to squelch the rumors.

Don't be concerned about overreacting. My bet is that if you have become aware of some negative word of mouth about your business, it's only the tip of the iceberg. The consequences of under-reacting, that is, of not doing enough to stop the bad word of mouth in its tracks, can be far more dangerous to the future of your business than those of overreacting.

Getting Started Tomorrow Morning

People generally tell long, involved stories only when they're relaying something bad that happened to them: "Lemme tell you about how so-and-so totally goofed up my order."

On the other hand, if people are going to say something nice, it's usually short, sweet, and to the point: "ABC Widget is good people to do business with!"

So, if your customers are going to talk to other people about you, what *one* thing would you want them to say about your business, your organization, your products, or your services? Try writing it down in twenty-five words or less, and preferably twelve words or less.

Now think of at least three specific ways in which you encouraged your customers to spread this positive image of you by word of mouth over the last six months.

Finally, think of three new ways you could encourage positive word of mouth.

13

Using Direct Mail to Promote to Existing Customers

This chapter and Chapter 14 are *not* about how you can go into the direct mail marketing business. Land's End, Blair, Eddie Bauer, Smith & Hawkins, Lillian Vernon, and REI, to name just a few, are all in the direct mail business. They publish major catalogs and/or fliers of one kind or another on a regular basis to sell you everything from preppy clothing to backpacks, from garden tools to fishing and hunting gear. Although they may have a few retail outlets, they mainly ask you to place your order through an 800 number, and the bulk of their sales are through catalog orders. How to get into the direct mail marketing business is beyond the scope of this book.

What this chapter *is* about is how you can use direct mail as a marketing tool to stay in touch with your customers. (How to use direct mail to help get new customers is discussed in Chapter 14.)

DIRECT MAIL TO EXISTING CUSTOMERS

Most small businesses that I'm familiar with need to pay much more attention to holding on to their existing customer base than they do. Why? Because an existing customer is worth his or her weight in gold!

A quick lesson in demographics: Over the last roughly forty years, the huge baby boom generation has dominated our economy. To a great extent, from 1945 to the late 1970s, a business could look forward to growth based on growth of the marketplace itself. In other words, the pie itself was getting bigger, so everybody's piece was consequently bigger.

Starting in the late 1970s, the baby boom tide began to turn. The overall marketplace was not growing, and some specific segments actually began to shrink. The result was that marketers interested in growing—and who isn't?—were forced to shift to a much more aggressive strategy, a strategy in which growth came from increased market share (a bigger piece of the pie). That bigger piece of the pie meant that someone else's piece was *not* as big.

In other words, instead of new customers simply coming from the larger population base, new customers had to be taken away from someone else.

That's why, in the highly competitive 1990s, holding on to your existing customers needs to be an essential part of your marketing strategy.

As far as your existing customers go, you can effectively use direct mail promotion to:

- Keep your name in front of them on a regular and frequent basis.
- Reinforce your marketplace position or image—what your business is in your customers' minds.
- Remind them about the unique products or services you offer—what makes you different from (read that as "better than") your competitors.
- Introduce new products or services.
- Update them on improvements to your products or services.
- Tell them about new ways to use your products or services.

The fact is, direct mail is a powerful marketing tool for staying in touch with and therefore helping cement a relationship with customers, clients, contributors, or members that is underutilized by most small marketers, and especially by nonprofit organizations.

For promotional purposes, paid media advertising is a little like one of those Gatling machine guns, spraying thousands of rounds in the general vicinity of the target and hoping to hit it just through sheer numbers. On the other hand, a direct mail promotional message can be like a rifle shot directed specifically at your customers and your customers only.

Direct mail material sent to your customers can take a variety of forms, each of which has unique strengths that make it good for specialized purposes. These can include newsletters, product bulletins or fliers, brochures, customer letters, and even postcards. Let's explore each one in a bit more detail.

NEWSLETTERS

A newsletter is just what the name implies: a regular publication of news and information sent to your customers. A customer newsletter has some distinct advantages over paid media ads:

- It can include much more information than you could possibly run in most print media ads (except, perhaps, a full page, if you could afford one) and certainly any electronic media ad (except, perhaps, a half-hour paid program, if you could afford one).
- It is certainly more specifically targeted, since by selecting the list you have complete control over who sees it.
- It is far less expensive than paid ads on a per customer per contact basis.
- It offers more flexibility in terms of visual format.
- Last, but by no means least, it can be far more personal.

Newsletters have some disadvantages you need to keep in mind:

- They can be rather time-consuming to produce, especially if you're doing it yourself. You have to gather the information and graphic materials, write and edit the newsletter, lay it out, take it to the printer, and, eventually, fool around with mailing labels, postage, etc.
- Newsletters are best used as a supplement to your overall advertising program, not as a replacement for paid media advertising. Using direct mail as a mass promotion technique, like media advertising, is very expensive, and I think it is definitely a step over the line that separates direct mail as a part

of your marketing program from direct mail as a business in its own right.

Customer Needs Are the Secret of Success

The secret to developing a successful customer newsletter is to make it responsive to your customers' needs, not yours. If your customers do not immediately see the relevance of the information in your newsletter to their everyday problems, they will not bother to read it. Of course, you can still give them information you want them to know, but you have to present and package it in such a way as to make them think they *need* to know this.

I'd recommend that you start out with a quarterly newsletter, perhaps published seasonally (Spring, Summer, Fall, Winter). Why not more frequently, like monthly?

• As I said, a newsletter can be time-consuming to produce. If you try to do it monthly, I can almost guarantee that after the third or fourth month you'll start dreading it. It will be a burden, and you'll starting cutting corners, filling space with fluff instead of solid information. And I can definitely guarantee that your readers will instantly detect this shift and will very quickly become former readers.

• Unless you're in some kind of highly volatile industry, like pork belly futures or computer chips, it's very tough to come up with enough good solid information to sustain a newsletter on a monthly basis.

• Unless you *can* come up with some really hot new stuff every month, your readers, who perceive themselves as busy and overworked, may begin to see your newsletter as more of a pest than a help. Then, when you do have good stuff to tell them, they'll tend to ignore it.

It's far better to get your feet wet, so to speak, by publishing less frequently, but still regularly. Experiment a bit; find out what your customers want to know and the form in which they would like to get it. Get comfortable with your own approach to producing a newsletter. Find out just how much good information really is available and how quickly and easily you can acquire it and convert it to usable material. Then, if your customers are really demanding it and if you find you can comfortably produce it, switch to bimonthly (every other month).

A Basic Newsletter Format

Your newsletter should start out with a single sheet of 8 ½ by 11 (letter size) paper, printed on two sides. If need be, you can go to an 8 ½ by 14 (legal size) page, printed on both sides.

It should have a set heading, usually referred to as a masthead, at the top of the first page that clearly identifies it, first, as a newsletter, and second, as *your* newsletter. This can be a variation of your regular letterhead. But it *must* include your business's or group's logo displayed prominently.

Now, about this business of selecting a name. For heaven's sake, call it what it is, a newsletter! Don't try to be cute or clever. Most of the time this effort at being creative ends up as some kind of pun or play on words that is entirely lost on customers.

You should set the copy in two columns per side, ragged right, which means unjustified. Your type should be no smaller than typical typewriter size, or about 9 or 10 points. Why? This is by far the easiest format for most people to read. This is also why I recommend sticking with more traditional type styles: These are the most reader-friendly.

One thing your newsletter absolutely *must* have is graphics—photos, drawings, graphs, charts, even clip art. If you can't or won't use graphics of some kind, don't bother publishing a newsletter; find an alternative. Why am I so adamant about using graphics? Because nearly forty years of television has conditioned most of us to expect information in a visually stimulating format. When we see nothing but copy, we are turned off. We're reminded of dull textbooks that are boring to read. This is not a conscious decision; rather, it's just a feeling.

Fold your newsletter two or three times, to an 8 ½-inch-wide by about 3 ¾-inch-vertical size. If you plan to use your newsletter as a self-mailer (in other words, not using an envelope), you should check the latest postal regulations.

By the way, I recommend that you use first-class postage on your newsletter for several reasons:

- If you use first-class postage, your newsletter gets first-class treatment, which means that it gets delivered in the most timely manner and you get address corrections if for some reason your customer has moved and didn't tell you.
- To qualify for a bulk rate, the post office has a minimum number of pieces (at this writing 250). Some small businesses, nonprofit agencies, and volunteer groups wouldn't necessarily send out that many newsletters.
- In order to qualify for the most favorable bulk rates, you need to do a lot of presorting, which can be both time-consuming and tricky if you aren't familiar with postal regulations.
- Bulk mail does not always receive the highest delivery priority. There are few things more annoying to your customer than to receive a newsletter announcing a special event *after* the special event is over.

About Style and Content

I can't urge you strongly enough to write your newsletter in an informal, conversational style. Second only to not having any graphics, a stiff, formal writing style is guaranteed to turn your readers off.

Never forget that a customer newsletter is a piece of sales literature. When you or your staff makes a sales call, is it stiff and formal? Or is it full of enthusiasm and excitement? Your newsletter should fairly brim with that same enthusiasm and, like any good sales pitch, should always focus on the benefit to the customer.

As far as what format the content will follow (one major article or lots of short items per issue), this will be governed to a great extent by the type of material you want to include—in other words, by the nature of your products or services and by the information needs of your customers. What follows is only a guideline for a typical newsletter.

Besides the masthead, half to two-thirds of the front page should consist of the major article of the issue, with at least one graphic element or photo. If the article is too long for this space, it can be "jumped" or continued on the back page. The remaining half to one-third of the front can be a second, shorter article, a self-contained photograph and caption, or some kind of indication of other articles on the back.

The back page of your newsletter might then include:

- The continuation of the article from the front
- A second, shorter article, preferably with a graphic
- News briefs, basically a series of one- or two-paragraph mini-articles
- A calendar of upcoming events
- People profiles about your staff, especially the customer service folks—with a photo, of course

Finally, when you're contemplating doing a newsletter, don't get so hung up on some ideal that you decide not to produce the newsletter if you can't reach it. It would be nice if your newsletter were designed professionally, written by a top-notch free-lance writer, and typeset so that it looked slick and professional. But don't worry if it isn't. This kind of sophistication is necessary only if you are publishing a newsletter as a business and asking readers to pay a subscription fee.

Remember the purpose of your newsletter. It's a way for you to stay in touch with your customers, clients, contributors, or members. What's more important than a flashy presentation is the fact that you do it, that you are trying to stay in contact with people who are important to you. What's more important than slick writing is a sense of your own sincerity coming through. In fact, some of the most successful newsletters I've seen are, by so-called professional standards, very hokey.

I can't think of a business or nonprofit agency or volunteer group that couldn't effectively use a newsletter as part of its overall promotional program.

PRODUCT BULLETINS

The product bulletin is a variation on the newsletter. Although some aggressive, promotion-oriented businesses might find it useful to use both, for most of the small businesses this book is written for, one or the other issued on a regular basis is enough.

The major difference between the two is that a product bulletin tends to focus on a single product or service, usually treating it in some depth, whereas a newsletter will typically deal with several topics.

A product bulletin is often much more "how to" oriented or

places a greater emphasis on technical information than a newsletter.

A product bulletin also has the advantage of not having a prescribed frequency. For example, at the beginning of a model year you could conceivably issue a product bulletin weekly, each one focusing on a particular model, then not put out another one for several months.

A product bulletin is especially useful as a vehicle for telling customers about product improvements, upgrades, or new applications.

Like a newsletter, your product bulletins should have a consistent visual format so that your customers will recognize that they are coming from you. However, a product bulletin can have even less of a professionally typeset and printed look than a newsletter.

A basic product bulletin could consist of your letterhead with "PRODUCT BULLETIN" centered on the first line and then some kind of headline telling what the bulletin is about: "New polymer adds 1,000 hours to widget's life." The text can be right off your typewriter or word processor printer.

Graphics such as photos, drawings, charts, and graphs are desirable and certainly recommended, but not mandatory.

Owners of businesses that deal in products or services that are highly technical, that have frequent model or design changes (annually is considered frequent for this example), or for which new applications (uses) are being developed on a regular basis might want to consider adding product bulletins to their promotional arsenal. This can include both retailers and manufacturers.

Remember that while both newsletters and product bulletins are mainly designed for distribution by mail, you can run off a few dozen (a few hundred?) extra copies and hand them out at your next trade show.

PROMOTIONAL FLIERS

When it comes to promotional fliers, imagination is about the only factor limiting who can use them, how they're used, and what they can look like.

What differentiates a flier from a product bulletin? Generally, promotional fliers are much more visually oriented and have less copy than a product bulletin. They use photos, drawings, cartoons, explosions, arrows, reverses, unusual type styles, or other graphic elements to create attention-demanding visual excitement.

A flier is typically used to announce a specific event, such as a sale, open house, grand opening, seminar, or product demonstration.

In most cases, a promotional flier ought to be a fairly close approximation of your print media ad announcing the same event, so that one reinforces the other.

For a real attention getter, try some unusual ink and stock color combinations—kelly green ink on canary paper, dark blue ink on shocking pink paper, deep red on lettuce green stock.

Use both sides of your flier. One side can give the essential information: the event title, time, date, and place, along with some dominant graphic, sort of like an ad (an 8 ½ by 11 sheet of paper is about the equivalent of a 4 by 11 newspaper ad). On the back you can add more detailed explanatory copy, perhaps with some additional graphics.

Finally, here are a few ideas for how to distribute a flier:

- Mail it stand-alone to your customer list.
- Insert it in your next newsletter.
- Stuff it in your customer statements.
- Insert it in your chamber of commerce newsletter (if it accepts inserts).
- Post it in prominent spots around your place of business.
- Drop it into customer packages at your checkout counter.
- Post it on bulletin boards at laundromats, supermarkets, drug stores, community centers, churches, or anywhere else they'll let you.

CUSTOMER LETTERS AND POSTCARDS

One of the simplest and yet most powerful ways to use direct mail as a promotional tool is to send your customers a simple letter or postcard, *especially* if you can give each one an element of personalization.

Here are some tips on using letters and postcards:

• Mail a printed postcard to your entire customer list to announce a special event, such as a sale or open house. To give it a more personal look, hand print the card and then have it duplicated, rather than having it typeset. If possible, personalize it even more by hand addressing it or by writing the customer's name on the front. Use it in addition to any media ads as a reinforcement.

• Send a printed postcard reminder to customers you haven't seen in a while.

• Use a postcard as a form of thank-you note to a new customer.

• Send out regular customer letters, as often as once a month if you like. This can be a useful alternative to a newsletter if you're uncomfortable with the more elaborate trappings of a newsletter. Instead of fretting about copy and graphics and setting type and the like, just sit down and "dash off" a gossipy note about what's going on with your business. I guarantee that your customers will comment about your letters.

• At the opposite end of the spectrum, write your customers a letter only once a year, perhaps in the form of a kind of annual report. In this case, its very rarity will demand attention.

By using a combination of these techniques, it's entirely possible for you to send your customers something at least six times a year, and perhaps as often as nine times—four seasonal newsletters, two or three product bulletins, two or three special event fliers or postcards, and one or two customer letters.

CAPTURE CUSTOMER NAMES AND ADDRESSES

Finally, everything in this chapter is based on the assumption that you *are* capturing the names and addresses of your customers in some form.

If you're not, then drop everything and start immediately. I don't mean after next month's sale, or when you can afford to hire an office girl to type labels, or when you can find the time to learn the mailing list application on your computer, I mean now. Period.

If you accept my theory, and it's by no means exclusively mine, that for most businesses growth will come by taking away somebody else's customers, if you are not capturing the names and addresses of your customers, you are literally giving your business away, customer by customer.

If you can put your customers' names on a computer and kick out mailing labels quickly and easily, great. But even if all you do is put them on index cards and you have to hand address all your mailings, hire college or high school kids to work after hours—it's worth it.

The most valuable thing you own, by far, is that list of customer names and addresses.

Getting Started Tomorrow Morning

Start a collection of newsletters, fliers, and customer letters and postcards.

First, scan your own mail for these items with a more sensitive eye. Are there any that strike your fancy? Why? Is it the visual presentation? Is it a catchy headline or clever graphic (maybe a cartoon or a picture of a pretty girl caught your eye)? Even if the item is something you would ordinarily throw out because it is something you have no need for, take a second glance and see if there are any ideas that might work for you.

Second, and this is an even more important and lucrative source, the next time you go to a state or national meeting of your trade association, start asking your colleagues if they use customer direct mail promotional techniques. My guess is that a majority will say that they don't, or that they do so only occasionally.

But I would also guess that you will run across one or two who are enthusiastic promoters of direct mail. These are the folks you want to latch on to. Pick their brains clean. I'd bet that they will willingly share all kinds of ideas because they will be so glad to have found someone who will listen to them. Ask them to send you samples of their most successful items.

If your trade group is into marketing, they might even have a seminar session on the topic of using direct mail to stay in touch with customers.

14

Using Direct Mail to Attract New Customers

Direct mail can also be a powerful marketing tool for attracting new customers. Why not just rely on paid media advertising? To understand the answer to this question, you need to think of where your business or organization falls on a kind of continuum.

At one extreme are the many businesses for which paid media advertising is the most appropriate method for taking their message to new customers, with direct mail used only in a supplemental role.

At the opposite extreme are businesses for which direct mail would be the most effective technique for reaching new customers, with media ads used only in a support role.

And for some businesses, it's about half and half.

How can you tell where your business or organization falls on this continuum? The key to the successful use of direct mail to attract new customers (and to figuring out where you fall on the continuum) is to understand how tightly targeted your customer group is. The more specifically you can define your customer group, the greater the likelihood that you can use direct mail as a marketing tool for new customers.

A dry cleaner and laundry with half a dozen locations scattered around an urban area would be placed well toward the end of the continuum that relies more on paid media advertising. Its customer profile is large and diverse—its potential customers include most adults of both sexes from a fairly broad age and income range, and they are geographically scattered throughout the community. This profile would strongly point toward using a lot of radio and/or TV to stress name identity and convenience of location, with regular newspaper coupon specials to attract new customers. A direct mail strategy for new customers might include occasional participation in a communitywide coupon mailer pack.

On the other hand, a company that specializes in installing, repairing, and maintaining nonmetal piping systems for the food processing industry would probably emphasize direct mail for new customer promotion. Its target market, compared to the dry cleaner's, is very tightly defined—it's the plant managers, maintenance supervisors, and purchasing agents for food processing operations. There are just so many food processing plants in a given area, and it's easy enough to find out who they are and where they are located, since they are almost certainly regulated by a state health or agriculture agency. It's easy for a marketer to simply call up each plant, find out the names of the key decision makers, and send them some kind of sales material in the mail, following up by phone later. In this case, the marketer would certainly not use any of the traditional local paid media, such as radio, TV, or local newspaper, but might legitimately consider running some paid ads in the trade publications read by the food processing industry.

Finally, a new general line insurance agent would probably use a more or less even mix of direct mail and media advertising to attract new customers. The agent might run a name-card-type ad—a four- or five-inch ad with a picture, major insurance company affiliations, types of insurance offered, and an address and phone number—in the newspaper on a regular basis, and perhaps be a regular sponsor of the morning weather report on a local radio station. In addition, the agent might also select demographic groups of particular interest—small businesses, people with young families, retirees—and mail them an introductory letter, perhaps promising them some small gift if they ask for an insurance quote.

GOALS AND EXPECTATIONS

What can you reasonably expect from a direct mail promotion directed at attracting new customers? There are only two possible goals:

1. Creating actual traffic in your place of business
2. Generating an inquiry, a name, which can then be followed up on later

This, in turn, raises another question: What kind of response can you expect from a direct mail promotion program directed at new customers? In direct mail the rule of thumb is:

- A 1 percent response is marginally adequate.
- A 2 to 3 percent response is considered a successful program.
- A 5 percent response is cause for celebration.

Doesn't seem like much, does it? But look at it in an overall promotional context.

First, except in rare cases, most TV, radio, or newspaper ad sales reps would be delighted if someone's ad campaign in their medium pulled a response of one-half of 1 percent—that is, if one out of 200 people who were exposed to the ad actually responded.

Second, paid media ads probably cost more than a direct mail program. This means that direct mail's cost per response would be lower. But this is true only for the tightly focused marketers we mentioned before. The cost of direct mail becomes prohibitive if you try to use it as a replacement for traditional media to reach a large and diverse audience.

If you've been thinking about it, this leads to yet another question: Should you spend more to get a new customer than the new customer will initially spend with you?

I'll answer that question with a question: What is a new customer worth to you, especially over time? "Over time" is the key element. Most magazine subscription marketers actually spend more to get a first-year subscriber than that first-year subscriber will pay them for the subscription. What the magazine is counting on is that a certain number of those first-year subscribers will become second-, third-, and even fourth-year subscribers and will, therefore, more than make up for what it cost to get them in the first place.

Here's a good rule of thumb to use to gauge how much you should spend for a new customer program, whether it uses paid media advertising or direct mail: If you can reasonably expect to recover the cost of getting that new customer in two years, give or take a few months, then it's probably worth doing.

BASICS OF SUCCESSFUL DIRECT MAIL

All you have to do is look at your own mail for a few days to get a feel for the incredible variety of tricks and gimmicks direct mail marketers use to get you to look at their stuff: $10 million sweepstakes, trips to exotic places, free gifts and premiums, bonuses, superslick four-color brochures, cleverly written sales letters, things to punch out or scrape off.

So how can your direct mail piece compete in such shark-infested waters with any hope of success? By remembering and practicing the basics:

• Contrary to popular belief, most people *do* look at all that so-called junk mail, especially if the envelope clearly gives them some indication that the contents are relevant to their work or personal lives.

It also helps significantly if a direct mail piece is from a recognizable local source, which is one of the major advantages you have over the big boys.

In your inside copy, whether on a brochure or sales letter, always remember the universal question that all customers ask as they're contemplating a purchase, even if unconsciously: "What's in it for me?" Stress specific and meaningful benefits—you'll save money or time, look more beautiful or handsome, be healthier, improve your sex life—and you'll at least get them to listen to your pitch.

• Remove all risk involved in responding. One of the biggest drawbacks of direct mail promotion is that if you're asking people to buy a product, they can't pick it up and try it. They can't check out its size or how well it's made or how the color will look on them. They're afraid they'll be stuck. Or, if you are asking them for an inquiry that you can follow up on, they're afraid they're going to be obligated to buy something.

Why do you think Land's End, one of the most successful and best-known direct mail marketers, has a simple two-word guarantee: "Guaranteed. Period."? If it doesn't fit, if the color looks bad on you, if you just don't like it, no problem; return it for a full refund, no questions asked.

Several times in your direct mail piece you should reinforce that you guarantee unconditional satisfaction or that there is no obligation to buy.

• A kind of corollary to removing all sense of risk is to provide lots of reassurance that people will be making the right decision if they decide to respond. Include testimonial quotes from enthusiastic customers, even the names of major, recognizable customers (check with them first to make sure it's okay). Talk about your longevity—you've been in business for five, ten, or more years, or you've sold thousands of these items. Mention the quality awards you've received or certifications you've achieved.

• Tell them the deal up front. Experienced direct mail marketers know that this is one of the first things that people will look at in a direct mail piece; then, if they are still interested in responding, they will go on to read the sales letter and brochure to get more information (translate that to read "looking for reinforcement that responding is a good decision").

So, don't frustrate the readers by making the particulars of the deal hard to find or difficult to decipher. You will *not* pique their curiosity so that they will respond to find out what the deal is. You'll just make them mad and they won't respond at all.

• Perhaps most important, ask them to take specific action. Why do you think all those mailers from the big boys have things you're supposed to scrape off to reveal whether you match the winning sequence or little puzzle pieces you're supposed to fit together to form a picture? They know that if they can get the reader involved in some activity, it's easier to get him or her to respond.

Ask your readers to take specific action:

—If you can't afford to include scrape-off cards or die-cut puzzle pieces, you can certainly include things they can check off, like answers to questions about which items they use most often or which products they want more information on.
—Include a postage-paid return postcard they can use to ask for more information. Tell them to mail it today.
—Tell them to dial your 800 number right now for answers to their questions.
—Urge them to bring in their discount coupon soon, while selections are best.

—If nothing else, promise them a cup of coffee and a smile if they drop in to see you at your store.

WHAT TO SEND

A direct mail marketing package to attract new customers can include one or more of the following items:

Sales Letter

This is essential. No new customer package should go out that does not include a sales letter written specifically for that purpose. Here are some guidelines for developing your letter. It should:

- Be a minimum of two sides of your 8 ½ by 11 letterhead and no longer than four sides.
- Stress specific benefits to the customer, which should be highlighted by being indented, by being underlined, or by being all caps.
- Clearly spell out how you are different from your competitors.
- Point out any guarantees you have.
- Mention testimonials of satisfied customers.
- Spell out what the deal is.
- Close with some specific action you want the reader to take.

As always, write in a clear, easy to understand, conversational style. Avoid like the plague any stiff or awkward phrasing and formal tone. If it sounds a little like Dick and Jane, it's okay. If you think it would have made your high school English teacher happy, toss it out and start over.

By the way, there's nothing wrong with the sales letter restating some of what's in your brochure.

Brochure

A brochure is optional to the extent that a small business trying to attract new customers could conceivably do an effective job with a good sales letter. (See Chapter 8 for a detailed discussion of how to design and develop copy for a brochure.) On the other hand, if you have a brochure about your business, send it along.

Coupon

A coupon is by far the most popular form of inducement to try to get new customers in. A few suggestions about coupons:

• If you're going to offer an across-the-board discount, make it a meaningful one—at least one-third off, and preferably half off. Look at it this way: If you offer a chintzy 10 or 15 percent off, you may always wonder whether your response was low because people weren't interested in what you were offering or because the inducement wasn't attractive enough.

There's nothing wrong with putting some qualifications on a coupon, such as a minimum purchase or that it can be used on full price items only, as long as you make them clear.

• Put a time limit on your coupon. If you're doing one large mailing, print the expiration date prominently right on the coupon. If you're sending out new customer pieces on a regular basis, a few at a time, hand stamp an expiration date on each one as you stuff it in the envelope.

The expiration date should be no farther off than a month or six weeks. If it's farther in the future, there's too much of a temptation for people to set it aside to use later, only to forget about it. An early expiration date on an attractive discount gives a sense of urgency.

• In lieu of an across-the-board discount, consider offering a specific item free just for stopping in, no obligation. It should be an item of at least $10 retail value, and perhaps as much as $20. And it should be an item with fairly universal appeal.

Again, while this might appear to be giving away the store, remember that your expectation should be that this is an investment with a long-term return.

Other forms of inducement besides a coupon include:

• An invitation to some kind of special event, such as an open house or private showing.
• An entry form for a drawing. If you do decide to try a drawing, have lots of prizes, which means lots of winners, even if you have to cut back on the grand prize to do it.

Finally, at the risk of repeating myself, I'll reinforce something here that I stressed in Chapter 13: Any coupon or other inducement piece should include a space for a name and address. *You want that name and address!* Even if your potential new customers don't necessarily buy now, you will add them to your mailing list and keep sending them your promotional material. You never know when you might hit their hot button with some promotion, or when they might become disgruntled with your competitor and decide to make a switch.

HOW OFTEN TO SEND MATERIAL

Except for the type of business that is heavily skewed toward using paid media ads to attract new customers, most small businesses should do some kind of new customer direct mailing at least once a year, with twice a year being the preferred option.

One of those mailings might take the form of a formal new customer packet, complete with sales letter, brochure, and inducement piece. But the second one could consist of the same postcard announcement of your annual clearance sale that you send to your regular customers.

There's a corollary question: How often should you send to the same list of potential new customers? You should send at least twice, and more often if the list very closely matches your customer profile.

If you send just one mailing, there's always the chance that it will get lost in the mail or that the potential customer will put it aside, intending to respond but never taking action. If you were making a personal sales call, you wouldn't quit after just one call, would you?

WHERE DO YOU GET LISTS?

Finding someone to send your new customer promotion packets to is the least of your worries. There are plenty of sources for names and addresses:

• You can do an occupant mailing to postal routes that are within a specified radius of your business.

• You can do an occupant mailing to postal routes in the more affluent part of your market area.

• You can buy commercial lists (the cost is roughly ten or twelve cents a name) from all kinds of list brokers. With sophisticated computers, it's incredible how specifically targeted commercial lists can be these days. Your phone book's Yellow Pages probably has local and out-of-town list brokers, or you can check at a local library for directories of list brokers.

• You can trade lists. Obviously, your head-to-head competitor probably won't want to trade customer lists with you, but there might be a complementary business that would—a children's clothing shop and a children's shoe shop might trade, a women's clothing shop and a nearby beauty salon might exchange, a massage therapist and a natural foods store might try cross mailings.

• You can build your own list. Watch the local newspaper, the local chamber of commerce newsletter, and any other sources you can think of for names of people who might be potential new customers.

Getting Started Tomorrow Morning

Get a sheet of notebook paper and divide it roughly into thirds horizontally.

In the top third, describe in no more than fifty words the group you think you get the bulk of your customers from. Use as many specifically descriptive words as you can—age, gender, family makeup, income, location, occupation, place of residence. Leave a few lines at the bottom of this third; we're going to come back to this section.

In the middle third, describe the next largest group from which you draw customers, and in the bottom third, the third largest group. As before, leave some space at the bottom of each section.

Now, go back and reread your description of the first group. Do you want to modify it in any way? In the space at the bottom of this section, give a percentage estimate (your best guess if that's all you can do) of the number of potential customers in your market area from this group.

Repeat this step for each of the other two sections.

This little exercise should have provided you with two results. First, it should give you at least a preliminary sense of what target groups you might logically look to for new customers. Second, it should spark some thoughts on where you might find names and/or locales to send new customer mailings to.

15

Staying in Touch
Is a Two-Way Street

A friend of mine lives in Florida. Not surprisingly, he and his wife have a lot of friends and relatives come to visit during the months of December, January, and February. My friend's wife is the sales manager for one of the larger housing developments in the area where they live. The development particularly targets retirees as its customers.

Whenever visitors stay for more than a couple of days, my friend's wife asks them to do her a favor. The favor is to go out to one of the other major housing developments and pretend they are interested in moving there.

When they are done, she takes them to lunch and picks their brains. What did you think of the looks of the houses? What did you think of the floor plans? What would you change about the houses if you could? How did you like the landscaping? How were you treated by the sales staff? Did they answer all your questions completely? Did they seem honest and sincere? Were they enthusiastic or bored? Were they too aggressive? What did you think of the prices of the homes? Do you feel you'd be getting your money's worth?

Sometimes she even has them visit her own development.

Of course, what she has done is create an informal network of secret shoppers. She's been doing this for years, and she has developed a very good base knowledge about what her customers and potential customers want and how they feel about her business and her competitors.

Why doesn't she just go and check out the other developments herself? After all, doesn't she know more about what to look for? Ironically, her disadvantage is that she knows too much about housing developments and about sales techniques to be able to think like a customer. She's too objective. That's right, too objective. What she's really looking for from her secret shopper friends is their subjective (as in personal) responses to her competition.

BE CUSTOMER-DRIVEN

I've seen more than a few lists of the reasons why businesses don't make it. They almost always include things like lack of sufficient capital, lack of experience in the field, poor initial planning, inability to manage the business properly, a poor economy, marketplace too small to support a business, and not enough promotion and advertising.

I have yet to see a list that includes "lost touch with its customers" as a reason for a business not succeeding. Yet, having worked with hundreds of small businesses over the years, I would rank that, along with a variation that might read something like "never able to establish touch with customers," among the top five real-world reasons why businesses, especially small businesses, don't make it.

A theme that I hammer at over and over in this book is that to be successful in today's overstored, overproducted marketplaces, a business must be customer-driven. The only way your business can be customer-driven is for you to be in touch with your customers and potential customers on a regular and frequent basis.

Being in touch with your customers is a two-way street. One way is for you to talk to them about your business and what it does and how it's different from the competition. This kind of outbound being in touch involves sending out newsletters and hosting special events, which are covered in Chapters 13, 14, and 16.

The other way of staying in touch with customers and potential customers is to have them talk to you, to have them tell you who they are, what they want and don't want, and how they feel about your business and your competition. This chapter will focus on ways you can develop this inbound channel of information.

FIND OUT WHO YOUR CUSTOMERS ARE

I don't care what kind of business you're in or what kind of nonprofit agency you run or what kind of volunteer organization you're involved with, you need to know who your customers are. Period. You need to know exactly who they are—their names, their addresses, their phone numbers, and as much about their lifestyles and other characteristics as you can find out.

The absolute minimum that you should be doing in order to stay in touch with your customers is collecting their names, addresses, and phone numbers. The names, addresses, and phone numbers of your customers are the single most valuable thing you own—more valuable, even, than your building or your inventory.

Where can you get these names, addresses, and phone numbers?

• You can get them from the checks customers write to you. Before you make your nightly deposit, put all your checks on your copier and make copies of the check faces. You can even overlap them so that all you see is the address.

• You can get them from credit card slips. Even if the card issuer doesn't require an address (after all, the issuer already has it on its computer), you should ask the customer to fill in his or her address and phone number.

• You can simply ask for them. There are several ways. Post a sign that says, "Would you like to be on our mailing list?" Right below it keep a supply of slips for customers to fill out with their name, address, and phone number.

Have a guest book for people to sign.

Have periodic prize drawings as part of a sale or special event, with a name, address, and phone number on the registration slip.

From time to time in your newsletter, include a little article or coupon asking your customers to suggest names of others who they think would be interested in being added to your mailing list.

If you have a computer with a mailing list software package, put these names and addresses in the computer. If you don't have a mailing list capability on your computer, look into getting a simple mailing list program. You'll be surprised at how inexpensive they've become.

If you don't have a computer, look into having someone who does have one keep your list for you. The first place to check is a local mailing house, someone who specializes in doing direct mail work. Another place to check is a small bookkeeping service that might be willing to keep a list for you, inputting the names and addresses and kicking out labels when you need them. You could also check with an office center that answers phones, types letters, and the like.

If you think you can't afford to have someone with a computer do your mailing list for you, keep the list manually. There are all kinds of inexpensive systems available at office supply shops that allow you to type names and addresses on a master form, then run off copies onto gummed labels.

Go Beyond Names and Addresses

Finding out who your customers are means more than just knowing their names and addresses. It means finding out who they really are. The marketing jargon term is *demographics,* which simply means learning about things like:

- *Gender.* What percentage of your customers are female? Male?
- *Age.* Are your customers mostly young? How young? Old? How old?
- *Occupation.* Blue-collar? White-collar? Professional? Retired?
- *Income.* Two incomes in the household? Low? Moderate? High?

The list can be just about endless, even delving into:

- *Current buying habits.* How often do they shop for food? Clothes? Hardware items? Gifts? Where do they shop for these things?
- *Anticipated buying needs.* When do they plan to buy a new car? When will the washer or dryer need to be replaced?
- *Media habits.* What newspapers and magazines do they read? Do they listen to the radio? Which stations? When? Do they watch the early or late evening newscast on TV? How often?

I can imagine what many of you are thinking about now, especially if you've already started your business and have just confronted the hard reality of never having enough time to do everything that needs to get done. You're probably thinking, "What is this guy, some kind of nut? Keeping people coming through the door and putting out brushfires is about all I've got time and energy for. Typing up some kind of demographic survey and compiling the results is certainly not very high on my 'to do' list."

I hear you. But I would strongly suggest to you that knowing as much as you can about your customers is very much part of "keeping people coming through the door."

I would also suggest that learning things about your customers beyond their names and addresses does not necessarily mean that you have to have some long, involved, expensive studies done. Here are some suggestions.

One of the simplest ways to find out interesting things about your customers is simply to count noses. Over the next two weeks, stop whatever you're doing for a time and just count the people in your business. Do this at least five or six times over the two weeks, maybe once on a Saturday and then at different times on weekdays. Count how many females and males there are. Make a best guess as to their approximate age. How many familiar faces are there? How many strangers? How many have kids in tow? How are they dressed, casually or in jackets and ties? You can learn a lot just by really looking.

A lot of colleges, and even some high schools, now offer marketing classes. You might approach the teacher of a marketing class to see if there is a student who would like a practicum project of doing some market research for you. Working with you and the marketing teacher, the student could design a short survey form, conduct interviews with your customers, and tally the results. You might even get lucky and find a student willing to do the project for class credit and perhaps a reference letter from you.

When you go to a doctor for the first time, you're asked to fill out a new patient form. Well, why not devise a new customer information form for your business? Of course, you should ask for the customer's name, address, and phone number, but you should be able to get most people to answer a half dozen or so additional questions. What those questions should be is up to you and depends on the kind of business you're in. A good place to start is to ask yourself what it would be helpful to know about your customers. Not everyone will be willing to fill out the new customer information form, but my prediction is that most will.

You might publish a variation of your new customer survey form in your newsletter once a year, asking readers to fill it out and send it in. The few duplicates you get from people who have already filled one out should be more than offset by the new information you'll be gathering.

Finally, you can also ask your media advertising representatives (TV, newspaper, and radio) for any market profiles they might have. Over the last several years the media in all but the smallest markets have become very sophisticated in developing profiles of local markets. While this information is not about your specific customers, it's better than no information at all, and it might give you some ideas on the kinds of information you want to develop from your customers.

FIND OUT WHAT YOUR CUSTOMERS LIKE AND DON'T LIKE

However, really staying in touch with your customers means asking them what they think of your business, asking them how they feel about your competition, and asking them how you could do a better job of meeting their needs. Here are some ideas.

For any kind of retail shop or service business, the absolute minimum you should be doing is putting out a classic suggestion box. Actually, there should be several of these placed throughout your business.

Post a sign above the box that asks, "How are we doing?" Supply a form and a pencil right alongside the box.

The form should contain nothing but blank lines to allow a completely open-ended response. You might also include an optional place for name, address, and phone number. Of course this is added to your mailing list, but you should also use it to follow up, either with a little note thanking the person for a positive suggestion or with a personal phone call to discuss a negative suggestion.

You can hand out customer response cards. Literally. A couple of times a year—for example, during your Christmas open house and midsummer clearance—print up some kind of survey card and hand it out to every third or fifth or tenth customer that walks through the door. Ask these customers to fill them in and drop them in your suggestion box before they leave. Encourage them not to take the card home. You want their first blush reactions, not something they've pondered over, and furthermore, very few of them will ever get mailed back.

These cards are different from your suggestion form. They should ask the customer to rate your business in specific areas, usually on some kind of scale ranging from "excellent" to "needs improvement." You should probably not include more than a half dozen questions, plus an optional name, address, and phone section. If you ask for more than a half dozen responses, it'll take too long and your participation will drop. If you really feel you need to ask for information on more areas, do two different surveys a year.

You can put a questionnaire in your newsletter. You can use the same questions as on your customer response handouts or make up completely different questions. It's up to you.

You can call people up on the telephone and ask them how you're doing. Although any business can use this technique, it's especially useful for the kind of business where customers rarely come to you, such as an appliance repair service.

I am not suggesting here that you mount some kind of massive phone survey, where that's all you do for four or five days. Rather, I'm thinking of a regular program of phoning customers and simply asking, "How are we doing?"

Think about it. If you have one salesperson working for you, and each of you phones just one customer a week (surely you can find the time to talk to just one customer a week!), that's a hundred customers a year. You can find out a lot of interesting things from a hundred customers. If you can find time to do more than one call a week, or every other week, that's 150 or more customers a year.

Finally, you can hold some informal focus groups. Big marketers do a lot of focus group work. Whereas a survey or questionnaire usually has specific questions to respond to, a focus group is more of an open discussion in which the participants interact. The purpose of focus groups is to get more qualitative, as opposed to quantitative, information—to explore the "why" behind how people feel.

Focus groups are especially useful for businesses that depend on staying in touch with changing trends or fashions, like a fashion clothing store.

A focus group should have eight to at most twelve members; if it has more, it gets too large to keep up with and too intimidating for good group interchange. It should probably not go on for more than an hour or an hour and a half. And you should probably schedule a minimum of three groups (thirty to thirty-six total participants) in order to get a cross section of your customers.

The focus group facilitator's job is to keep the group on task, to make sure everyone is heard from, and to seek clarification or expansion of ideas. The facilitator should not try to take voluminous notes about what is being said. Rather, someone else, who is not part of the discussion, should take notes, or the facilitator should simply tape-record the discussion and prepare a summary later.

Finally, a focus group is *not* a forum for the owner or manager to explain or defend what the business is doing. A focus group is for listening!

FOR HEAVEN'S SAKE, LOOK AT THE RESULTS!

I am regularly amazed at the number of businesses I discover that have some sort of customer questionnaire, but hardly look at the results. At best, they use the questionnaire as a kind of red flag system, designed to alert them to some negative that needs immediate fixing.

I worked with a business that had been collecting customer response cards for close to four years. Each month it tallied up that particular month's answers and looked for any specific problem areas that needed attention. But it had never done a comparison of the results over time, which would reveal any trends. And, even more amazingly, it had never looked at what positives the customer responses had identified.

The business was a motel, restaurant, and mini-convention center. One of the first things I did in working with it was to take the old customer response cards (thank heaven the business had saved all of them!) and plot the results over the nearly four years. I focused on the positives, as well as the negatives. Here are just two of the surprising results that were found:

1. The number of people who specifically mentioned that a way to improve the facility was to have a fitness room of some kind, while small, was slowly increasing in both numbers and frequency. Al-

though this was not a problem that needed immediate attention, it did reveal a trend that seemed to be growing in importance to at least some of the facility's customers. The facility decided to add an exercise room to its three-year expansion plans.

2. Looking at the positives revealed another interesting trend. Over the nearly four years, the one aspect of the facility that was most consistently rated high and that elicited the most frequent specifically positive comments was its cleanliness. When I mentioned this, the reaction was, "Well, okay, as long as the cleanliness rating doesn't slip, we're happy." Yet that consistently high rating, and especially the unsolicited comments, suggested to me that the facility had a major hidden strength in its cleanliness that could be used to help differentiate it from the competition. It was decided that when the promotional brochure about the facility was reprinted, a section about the careful attention to cleanliness would be added.

I'm sure my point is obvious. Use the information your customers are giving you—not just to alert you to short-term problem areas, but to reveal long-term trends and, even more important, to identify any hidden strengths you might have.

Getting Started Tomorrow Morning

At a minimum, start a collection of customer response cards and questionnaires. Every time you spot one, first, fill one out for the business, and second, pick one up for your file. If you've never looked before, you're going to be surprised at how many you see. Especially look for them in businesses in your industry.

The next time you're at a regional, state, or national convention for your industry, ask your colleagues for copies of their customer response questionnaires. Ask your national trade association if it has designed a model customer questionnaire.

After you've collected a dozen or so, look them over. Read the questions. My suspicion is that you'll find that the areas in which they ask for information are very similar, even when the customer response surveys are from different industries. I also suspect that you will see some patterns in the scales customers are to use to rank their response.

And I suspect that for may of the questions, you'll find yourself thinking, "Yeah, I'd like to know how my customers feel about that," or, "Boy, it'd sure help me if I knew what my customers' attitude was about such-and-such." Congratulations; you've just taken the first major step toward developing a customer response questionnaire for your business.

However, since collecting these sample questionnaires and studying them and designing your own and getting it printed will take some time, and since getting in touch with your customers should not be put off for three or four or six months, here's the second part of your assignment. Start phoning a minimum of three customers each week and asking them how you're doing. If you have salespeople, have them phone no less than two or three a week as well.

The first reaction you're going to get when you start these calls is disbelief. No one ever calls up customers just to ask how he or she is doing. Your customers will think this is a back-door way of asking for an order or that you're going to pitch some new product. Reassure them that this is not the case, that you're truly just interested in how they feel about your business.

Once they're convinced that this is not just a sneaky way to make a sales pitch, the second reaction you'll get is probably something noncommittal like, "Well, you're doing just fine." To find out what you really want to know will take some gentle but persistent probing. Make sure each of the phone interviews includes the following three questions:

1. *Do you like doing business with us? Why?* This question is designed to get at your strengths from the customers' point of view.
2. *Do you have any needs we are not now meeting? How could we meet those needs?* This question should help reveal any opportunities for new products or services you might be able to offer.
3. *Is there anything we can do to better serve you?* This question should help identify any specific weaknesses in your business.

16

Special Events

Remember when you felt close to the people you did business with? You could walk into their stores or offices and they knew your name and you knew theirs. And, equally important, they probably knew from memory what size you wore and what colors you preferred.

We hear again and again about how impersonal our relationships with our customers are becoming. In the name of speed and efficiency (translate that as cost savings), the computer now scans our preferred customer card and remembers that we like gel toothpaste rather than traditional and that we buy 1.7 gallons of 2 percent milk per week, on the average.

From a marketing standpoint, customers are increasingly becoming inhuman collections of numbers—brand preferences, buying frequencies, demographic data—instead of living, breathing people with identities and feelings.

Staging a special event can be an excellent opportunity for a business or organization to recapture, even if temporarily, that feeling of a personal relationship with people who are important to it.

Special events are activities like an open house, an anniversary celebration, a tour, a show, a workshop or demonstration, an all-night sale, a party, or an appearance by a VIP.

Keep in mind that we are talking here about special events specifically for your customers, clients, members, or contributors, a defined group of people who are important to your business or organization.

WHY DO SPECIAL EVENTS?

Special events certainly represent a significant investment of work and, in some cases, money. Why focus all that time and money on a relatively few people? Why not use the money for more paid media ads or a direct mail campaign that will certainly reach more people?

The selectivity, the limited focus of a special event is the very essence of the reason for doing one. A special event is an intense, one-on-one relationship with a customer or someone who is important to you.

Remember that we are talking here in relative terms. An advertising campaign or a direct mail effort is designed to reach large numbers of people—its potential contacts may be measured in thousands or even tens of thousands. However, the impact of an ad or direct mail piece on any given individual may be relatively low— the people you want to reach weren't watching TV at the time your ad is on, or they didn't pay much attention to your direct mail piece because it arrived on the same day as a half dozen bills.

A special event, on the other hand, although intentionally directed at a more limited number of people, can have a significantly greater impact on each individual that participates. This brings us to the goals of special events:

- The number one goal of a special event is to create a feeling of individual—and I emphasize the word *individual*—importance for your customers, to make them feel special.
- A corollary goal is to create an intense relationship between you and these important people, to be memorable, to develop a lasting impression.
- Another major goal is to differentiate your business from the competition—to make your business or organization number one in the customers' minds.
- Finally, if yours is a well-established business, staging regular special events can be an important component in your strategy to hold on to your market share, to keep your customers.

Did you notice that these goals said nothing about numbers, about turning out large crowds? Media advertising and direct mail campaigns are about numbers. Special events are not about numbers, they're about relationships.

You may also have noticed that none of the goals said anything about selling. Certainly you can and should sell things at a special event: your products, your services, your organization. But, once again, if the only reason for your special event is to have a sale, then you have tapped into only one narrow aspect of the real potential of special events.

OPPORTUNITIES FOR SPECIAL EVENTS

With just a little imagination, most organizations could, I think, easily find a half dozen or more valid reasons a year for having a special event. This is not to say that you should necessarily stage all of them; perhaps just pick the two or three that offer the best opportunity to touch your customers in the most meaningful way.

You can put on a special event anytime you introduce something new:

• Your grand opening. This is probably the single most common special event.

Start your grand opening with limited-invitation VIP tours. Have one for the local chamber of commerce members, maybe another for a merchants' association, and perhaps another for your business luncheon club or some other group you can specifically identify as being important to you.

Then issue general invitations through media ads and/or direct mail promotions to anyone who wants to come.

• When you introduce a new line of products or services. This is probably the next most popular special event for most organizations. These can include trunk showings, fashion shows, and exhibitions and demonstrations of all kinds.

If you're going to have a news conference to announce a major new product or service, invite VIP customers to be in the audience. This will impress the media and will make the attendees feel special. Follow the news conference with some refreshments.

• When you open a new location or expand or remodel your present location, including adding any new major equipment. Strut your stuff with a tour, open house, or demonstration.

Any milestone event for your organization is an opportunity to put on a special event:

- A birthday or anniversary, especially a major one, such as your tenth or fiftieth. What a good excuse to not only show off your building and your products, but reinforce to your customers your staying power and how you're different from the competition.
- Reaching an important plateau, such as getting your 10,000th customer or becoming Number One in a market. It's a great way to reinforce your success.

You can revolve a special event around showing off a VIP of some kind. Certainly this can mean a celebrity, if you're lucky enough to have Robert Redford or Elizabeth Taylor as a relative who will come out of the goodness of his or her heart. But it doesn't just mean Hollywood stars. For example, it can be someone who has accomplished something important within your industry, like an Olympic medalist who does a tour under the sponsorship of a major athletic shoe manufacturer.

A celebrity can be a local winner of some kind. Every year a local bank holds a reception for the individual school winners of spelling bees. Hundreds of parents and relatives attend.

It can be a visiting executive of a prominent manufacturer in your industry. A local bike shop created traffic jams when the vice-president of a major Japanese bike manufacturer visited one Saturday afternoon.

In fact, the celebrity doesn't even have to be human. An elephant borrowed from a local zoo is the star attraction at a lawn and garden show. Did you know that elephant doo is one of the finest rose fertilizers? Apparently the crowds who show up at the show know.

The seasons and holidays offer ample opportunity for putting together a theme special event.

- Why not have an all-night sale on Halloween, complete with costumed employees, refreshments, and hourly giveaways?
- If your name is O'Connor or O'Rourke, why not host a St. Patrick's Day party for your customers, complete with food and green bunting?
- If your business is a garden center or you sell camping gear, why not offer a series of free, by-invitation how-to workshops

during the last week in February, when everyone is tired of winter and looking forward to spring?
- Why couldn't a beauty shop, a women's ready-to-wear shop, a women's shoe shop, and a travel agency all combine forces to stage a Great Getaway Night in the fall, including displays and exhibits about cruises and tropical resorts, a fashion show of cruise wear and sportswear, and tips for makeup and hair styles?

SOME KINDS OF SPECIAL EVENTS

The irony is that there are only a half dozen basic kinds of special event—an open house, a reception, a party, a tour, an exhibit or showing, and a seminar or workshop. But, just as there are only a few basic moves in chess and the excitement of the game is in the infinite variations of those moves, the fun of special events is the variations on the basic kinds. Let's look at each one.

Open House

An open house is probably one of the easiest and most common special events because there is relatively little structure. Essentially, you just throw open your doors so that people can visit. Of course, there are special activities, tours, displays, food, and so on. But part of the point of an open house is to show off your organization's operations in a more or less typical mode.

The grand opening of your business or organization is one example of an open house.

In general, though, the open house probably works better for organizations that are not normally open to the public, such as a manufacturer or a human service agency, since there is a built-in curiosity factor involved.

Reception

Hosting a reception generally revolves around a "celebrity" or a special occasion. I put quotes around "celebrity" because, once again, this doesn't mean you have to have Jack Nicklaus or Martina Navratilova show up.

A celebrity can be your organization's new CEO that you want your customers or clients to get acquainted with. A celebrity can be the director of your national trade organization or advocacy group. A celebrity can be the author of a book or manual that's relevant to your field.

A reception can be combined with other events. For instance, as part of a day-long open house, you might schedule a special reception at a specific time to officially greet the new CEO.

Tours

If I were running an organization that involved any type of gee-whiz equipment—a manufacturing plant of just about any kind, a research or testing laboratory, an environmental cleanup operation, an automated warehouse or distribution center, a custom repair shop (the list is practically endless)—I'd take a customer on a tour of the place every time he or she came to visit, and I would certainly schedule a special customer tour day at least once a year.

A tour is an outstanding opportunity to both create an intense one-on-one relationship with a customer and point out the advantages of doing business with you (translate that to read: why you're better than the competition).

A suggestion: Whether you do tours regularly or just on a special day, have front-line people prepared to talk to the customers, perhaps giving a brief explanation of what they do, but especially pointing out how they take special care to do a quality job or to be responsive to customer needs.

Parties

There's nothing wrong with a business or organization just having some fun—having a celebration on its anniversary each year or when it passes some major milestone. That's the basic thrust of having a party for your customers.

When you have a party and bill it as a party, you need to make sure the fun aspects are in the forefront—food, entertainment, decorations, smiles. But there's no law that says you can't also display your products, pass out literature about your services, or offer tours of your operation.

Exhibits and Shows

Exhibits and shows are, in a sense, the opposite side of the same coin. In an exhibit or show, your products or services are the center of attention.

This category of special event offers a broad array of opportunities:

- You can rent an exhibit hall, either in your home town or out of town, to demonstrate your products.
- You can stage a fashion show, or you can ask a number of designers to do trunk showings.
- You can invite representatives of different manufacturers to do product demonstrations and answer customer questions.

Seminars and Workshops

This is one of the newest forms of special event. The insurance and financial services industries have discovered the value of seminars and are working this category with great success. But other fields have not jumped on the bandwagon as quickly, which means that there may be a real opportunity for you to get your foot in the door in your area ahead of your competition.

A case in point, my own: I do consulting with individual businesses on marketing communications and promotions. Other than direct referrals, the best source of new clients that I have, by far, is workshops and seminars. Sometimes up to a year or more after a seminar, I will get a phone call: "Hello, this is so-and-so. You probably don't remember me, but I attended one of your workshops, and I think you might be able to help me." And the person then goes on to explain the project.

Think about it for a moment. Isn't your industry changing? Aren't new technologies or new products emerging on a regular basis? Aren't new applications or new techniques for doing things being discovered all the time? Aren't there all sorts of new regulations coming down? Isn't there new market research data available? What do your customers want to know? Don't you have some (much?) of that information that you can share?

You can put a seminar together yourself, or you can contact industry trade groups and your major suppliers, who have access to experts that travel around to put on workshops and seminars.

Sales

Most retailers I know hold at least two sales a year, and some have almost continuous sales. So what's the difference between a regular sale and a special event sale?

A regular sale involves cutting prices either on selected merchandise or across the board to clear inventory or generate traffic. You advertise the fact that you're having a sale, and the in-store promotion is pretty much limited to some signs and banners.

On the other hand, a special event sale has a very strong element of the unusual, the unique:

- Staying open all night, with super specials every hour, and perhaps drawings and giveaways
- Tent sales, which may include food, clowns and jugglers, and even pony rides
- Auctions, complete with a fast-talking auctioneer

SECRETS OF A SUCCESSFUL SPECIAL EVENT

There are three interrelated secrets to the success of a special event for customers. The first is to understand that in the customer's view, your special event is as much an entertainment as it is conducting business. The second is to make your customers feel special, important. And the third is that the event must be right for you. Let's explore each a bit further.

That your event is seen as an entertainment may not be something that has occurred to you. As I said in Chapter 2, it is a myth to assume that everyone makes buying decisions based on purely rational thinking. If you think your customers will readily see the rational value of coming to your event because you have important information for them, your special event is probably going to be a flop.

I would suggest that the degree to which you can inject elements of fun, of entertainment, into your special event will be the degree to which you can get people out. To paraphrase the movie *Field of Dreams*, make it fun and they will come.

So, what does fun mean?

• It means refreshments. They can be as simple as coffee and cookies, as elegant as a big spread of hors d'oeuvres, or as down home as hot dogs and soda. Food is an essential ingredient if people are to have fun. And the more festive you can make it, the better.

By the way, alcohol is optional. In fact, with today's more responsible approach to alcohol, wine would be the most I would offer in most cases.

• It means having some kind of entertainment, usually music. At a minimum I'd have a boom box playing background music. Better yet would be to have a live roving violinist or a guitarist or piano player.

• It certainly means decorating your place. Put up some colorful bunting. Hang festive banners. Put out vases of fresh flowers.

• It can also mean dressing up in costume. While Halloween is an obvious time for costumes, why not use your imagination? If you're celebrating your organization's fiftieth anniversary, why not have everyone dress in 1940s clothes? If you're announcing a major remodeling, have a "this place is going to be a zoo" party and have everyone dress up in animal costumes.

Turning to the second secret of success for special events, how do you make customers feel special or important?

• Whenever possible, send personally addressed invitations. (That's not so hard when you already have your customers' names and addresses.)
• Better yet, hand deliver your invitations. A local hotel wanted to have an open house after a remodeling, so it issued "summonses" and had them hand delivered by a local uniformed security service.
• Forget the name tags. Yes, it's important for people to be addressed by name. But remember, these are supposed to be

your customers, people known to you. Having to use name tags sends the wrong message.

- Tell your staff to make a special effort to introduce the customers they know to other members of the staff.
- Get out from behind any display tables you might have. A display table at the front of a booth is like a barrier that separates you from the customer. Once again, it definitely sends the wrong message.
- Discourage your staff from standing around talking to one another. Tell them that they are expected to circulate and talk to customers. The only time one staff member should be talking to another is when introducing a customer.
- Except for an actual reception that has been billed as such, avoid formal reception lines.
- Give your customers a gift of some kind to take away with them—a nice pen with your business's name on it, an imprinted coffee mug, a commemorative medallion paperweight, a T-shirt.
- If the occasion calls for some kind of welcoming talk or speech, don't hide behind a podium, which is another kind of barrier. In your talk, make frequent references to customers by name. Tell humorous anecdotes about yourself and your staff.
- And lots of smiles and handshakes should be the order of the day.

Finally, what do I mean when I say that in order for an event to be successful, it has to be right for you?

Whether you realize it or not, every organization is a reflection of the collective personalities of the people who operate it, from the CEO right down to the front-line folks. More by instinct than by conscious thought, they know what kind of special event will fly and what won't, both with the organization itself and with the customer group.

All I'm suggesting here is that when you're planning a special event, you should pay attention to your collective instincts. In fact, it's the smart CEO or manager who, when looking for ideas for a special event, asks for and listens carefully to ideas from his or her front-line people.

Getting Started Tomorrow Morning

First, start a list of excuses for having a customer special event. Do you have a major anniversary coming up? Are you planning any kind of remodeling or expansion? Do you have some new equipment coming in? Is there a major new line of products about to be announced? Are you about to introduce a new service? Or is there just some fun thing that you think would fly with your customers?

Second, gather your staff together and explain to them that you want to do some kind of customer special event. Ask them for their ideas and suggestions. Were any of their ideas similar or at least parallel to yours? Then you might well be on to something.

17

Advertising Specialties

In the trade they're called advertising specialties. They include everything from calendars to coffee mugs, frisbees to balloons, key rings to stadium blankets, ballpoint pens to commemorative coins, notepads to briefcases, caps, T-shirts, warmup jackets, bowling shirts, and baseball uniforms. In other words, just about anything you can put your business's name on can be an advertising specialty.

Should your business or group be using advertising specialties? The answer is an unqualified yes. There's no doubt that you should be using some form of advertising specialties. The real question is which ones you should be using and when you should use them.

WHAT'S THE GOAL?

The decision as to which advertising specialty to use and when needs to grow out of what you want to achieve—in other words, your goal.

The basic goal of advertising specialties is to keep the name of your business in front of your customers and potential customers. In today's hypercompetitive marketplace, you need to understand that your customers can, in all probability, get the same things or nearly the same things they get from you from someone else. So it is very much in your best interest to keep reminding people that you're around.

In the arsenal of promotional tools available to small businesses, advertising specialties are a relatively inexpensive and yet very effective way to regularly reinforce your relationship with your customers and to help establish name recognition with noncustomers.

By the way, I hope you've noticed how carefully I've used words like *reinforce* and *remind*. Advertising specialties should never be considered a replacement for a regular media advertising program. They are only an adjunct to paid ads or other promotions.

For example, I would encourage the owner of a small-appliance repair shop to buy magnetic versions of its business card and pass them out to anyone who comes to the shop. When people put them on the refrigerator, if and when they have an appliance break down, they will immediately look for the magnet with the shop's number on it.

I would also encourage the owner of that same shop to pass out those magnets at a home show where it had a booth to people who stopped by to look at the booth. I would also encourage the shop owner to pass out a brochure about the business.

But I would not encourage that same owner to direct mail those business card magnets all over town, because this is stepping over the line into trying to use an ad specialty in place of media advertising.

CHOOSING YOUR ADVERTISING SPECIALTY

In choosing an advertising specialty, the problem will not be to find enough items to pick from. Rather, it will be trying to choose the right one from the incredible variety that is available. All you have to do is talk to any ad specialty sales rep and he or she will produce catalogs as thick as a large city's phone book filled with hundreds, if not thousands, of items. How do you choose from all that stuff?

When you're thinking about buying an ad specialty item for any reason, ask yourself two questions. The ideal item will qualify under both:

1. What specialty item strikes your fancy? It's quite possible you already have an item in mind, something that just occurred to you out of the blue or perhaps something you saw used effectively in a similar situation elsewhere.

Pay attention to those instincts; they are probably telling you something. If yours is an established business, or even if you are just in the startup phase but have experience in the industry, you probably have a feel for your customers. You know what's going to strike a responsive chord with them and what isn't.

2. Ask yourself what your customers are likely to use on a regular basis. And think of "use" in the broadest sense of the word, as in being kept around and seen in one form or another on a frequent basis.

The classic coffee mug is a case in point; it generally goes into your customer's break room or kitchen cabinet and gets used, and seen, on a daily basis. But a commemorative plaque or paperweight that finds its way onto a den wall or office coffee table and is seen on a more or less daily basis is also used.

When you're thinking about how people use items, think creatively as well. For example, how many shopping mall or athletic event parking lots have you driven through where you saw lots of cars with those folding sunshades wedged in the windshield or the rear window? Imagine how many people might see your business logo if you gave away those sunshades as part of some kind of spring promotion.

HOW AND WHEN TO USE AD SPECIALTIES

There are lots of specific uses for advertising specialties. Let's explore just a few.

Far and away the most prevalent reason most businesses or groups buy advertising specialties is simply to keep their name in front of people. In fact, I can't think of any business that should not have at least one item of this type always in stock.

For example, how many times have you been approached by some community group looking for a donation to help its fundraising ice cream social or casino night? Instead of a gift certificate, which only one person sees, why not donate imprinted pencils or pens or notepads or magnets or napkins or paper cups, which lots of people will see?

For most organizations, ad specialty items do not need to be top-of-the-line—unless, of course, you happen to run an exclusive men's wear shop on Rodeo Drive in Beverly Hills and your definition of a cheap suit starts at $1,000.

Similarly, many community groups will also be looking for door prizes or prizes for drawings. Again, instead of a gift certificate, which will be seen by only one person, why not contribute several coffee mugs or pen and pencil sets or baseball caps or golf visors or T-shirts? The out-of-pocket cost to you is comparable, and there is real value in your business's name being seen again and again, both at the event itself and on a continuing basis afterward.

Another excellent use of advertising specialty items is as a reward, either for your employees or for your customers. For instance, a salesperson who reaches a certain volume might receive a high-quality pen and pencil set with your company imprint. Or a customer who makes a referral that leads to a new account might be given an imprinted leather legal pad folder, complete with calculator, as a thank you. I know several real estate agents who regularly give a framed art print to a customer who has bought a house through them.

A variation on this theme is to use ad specialties as a commemorative item—for instance, to mark a significant anniversary or some major milestone. This can take the form of an everyday useful item, like a key ring or coffee mug, or it can be something special, such as a print of a specially commissioned watercolor painting or a commemorative plate. And, again, these can be distributed to employees and to customers.

Last, but not least, any new business should definitely use at least one advertising specialty item as part of its initial promotional strategy (read that as establishing its name identity).

Some examples:

- A new golf shop might give away imprinted golf umbrellas or imprinted knit shirts to the first 200 customers to come in
- A human service agency introducing a new volunteer befriender for senior shut-ins might distribute tie bars for men or lapel pins for women with the project's heart-shaped logo
- A new copy and quick print shop might distribute business cards that have been die cut to fit into a desktop card file
- A new plastic injection molding manufacturer might distribute imprinted foam plastic iced tea and lemonade picnic jugs.

Getting Started Tomorrow Morning

This one's an easy assignment. Basically, it's designed to get you to notice who uses advertising specialty items and how they use them.

Look around your business or office. How many imprinted items do you find? Note pads? Calendars? Pens and pencils? Legal pad holders? Pocket calculators? Coffee mugs? Desk organizers?

Make a list of all the items you find and who they are from. If there aren't at least a dozen, you're not looking very carefully. I wouldn't be surprised if you found two dozen or more without much effort.

Now look around your home. How many imprinted items do you find there? T-shirts, sweatshirts, and windbreakers? Umbrellas? Coffee mugs or glassware? Yardsticks? Paint stirrers? Treated lens cleaning cloths for your glasses? Plastic pitchers or jugs for iced tea? Tote bags for your trips to the grocery? Duffle bags for your trip to the athletic club? Wall or desk calendars? How about all those items in your utensil drawer?

Make a list of what you find and who the items are from. My guess is that you will find as many, if not more, imprinted advertising specialties in your home as at your business.

Now go back over your two lists. Put a circle around all the items that are from folks you regularly do business with. Again, I'd be surprised if you haven't circled at least half of the items on the lists, and probably more.

18

Writing a Marketing Plan

A marketing plan for General Motors or Coca-Cola fills several thick notebooks—and this is for just one product, because each individual product gets its own marketing plan.

There will be pages and pages of information on the target audience, demographic analyses of who buys the product and why—age, income, where they live, occupation, how they spend their leisure time, and, naturally, lots of data on which media they prefer.

There will be pages and pages of information on how the company will promote the product, descriptions of the creative concepts behind the promotions, storyboards for TV ads, mockups of newspaper and magazine ads, drawings of point-of-sale displays, and, of course, complex charts of media purchases, including which network programs the ads will be on and which print media they will appear in.

There will be pages and pages of information on how the product will find its way into the marketplace: how it will be distributed, what stores it will be in, and how it will get shelf space allocations.

There will be pages and pages of economic data: detailed information on the cost of manufacturing, distributing, and promoting the product and lengthy analyses of the expected sales trends, market share, and profitability of the product.

And, if this were a marketing plan for a new product being introduced into the marketplace, you could add 50 percent to the length of the plan.

Fortunately, a marketing plan for the kind of business this book is written for, a small, more or less local business run by a hands-on owner or manager, does not have to be anywhere near as complicated or as lengthy. In fact, to write a marketing plan for your small business or nonprofit agency, all you have to do is answer six basic questions about your business and your audience and provide revenue and expense projections and action plans. The six questions are:

1. Who are we?
2. What do we do and why do we do it?
3. Who do we do it for and why do we do it for them?
4. What could prevent us from doing it?
5. How will we promote our business?
6. How will we know if we are successful?

That's it. That's all you have to do to write your own marketing plan. It does not need to be a long, arduous, time-consuming task. In fact, you and your staff could certainly write it during a one-day— possibly even a half-day—brainstorming session.

ANSWERING THE QUESTIONS

Before we dive into the six questions, there are some things you need to keep in mind:

• Answer the questions in order. Don't skip around, and don't leave any out. How you answer a later question is very dependent on what you say to an earlier one.

For example, the question about how you will promote your business comes very near the end. This is because how you promote (whether you use radio rather than TV, or print rather than electronic media, or, for that matter, whether you even use that much paid media, as opposed to direct mail) is very dependent on how you answer previous questions, such as who your target audience is, what image you're trying to get across, and whether yours is a new business or a well-established business.

• As you get to the answers to later questions, you'll notice some overlap between them. For example, several questions ask you to analyze why you're doing something. In answering these why questions, you'll probably find yourself giving various descriptions of the market niche you're serving. This is okay. As far as I'm concerned, all this is doing is once again reinforcing how interrelated the various elements of marketing are.

• The questions are written as if they concerned an established business, so the answers will generally be in the present and to some degree in past tense. If yours is a new business or one that is still in the planning stage, you should simply rephrase the questions so that your answers are in the future tense.

• Not every example question that I use for each major question is necessarily going to apply to your individual business. I've done a little shotgunning here; that is, I've asked lots of different questions in order to try to cover as many bases as possible. At least think about each question, although in some cases you may simply answer that it does not apply.

• The answer to each major question should not be more than two handwritten pages (one side only) or one single-spaced typewritten page—say between 400 and 500 words. Some can be less. This means that your entire marketing plan, not including your action plans and budget projections, would be no more than twelve handwritten pages or six typewritten pages long, and no more than 1,200 to 1,500 words in length.

You might ask: Well, if big corporations develop these excruciatingly detailed marketing plans, shouldn't a small business's marketing plan be just as detailed, only on a smaller scale? The answer is no.

For one thing, it's been my experience that most small businesses have at best what I call a seat of the pants marketing plan. For an established business, the marketing plan usually consists of doing this year what was done last year—"Uh oh, July's coming up; we'd better start putting together our midsummer clearance." For a new business, the marketing plan unfortunately often consists of whatever is suggested by the first media sales rep through the door.

For another thing, it's a matter of balance. The real-world truth is that if I suggest to the overworked hands-on owner or manager of a small business that he or she needs to develop a lengthy and detailed marketing plan, it simply won't get done. It will always be in the process of getting done, permanently relegated to a back burner because of more immediate problems that need to be addressed.

Perhaps I'm oversimplifying a bit, but I don't think by much. In my view, even a basic marketing plan, if it's carefully thought out, is better than no plan at all.

Who Are We?

This first question is by far the most important question because it is the foundation upon which the answers to every other question build. If you fudge on this question, it's like building on a foundation of sand.

This is the overview description of your business. But be careful; this is *not* the place to get bogged down in a lot of detail on *what* your business does—that is covered in the next question. Rather, this is the section where you talk about who you are as a business.

Here is a series of questions that might be addressed to one degree or another in this section of your marketing plan:

- What does the business do? Is the business a retail operation? What category of product does it sell? Is it a manufacturer? What general line of products does it make? Is it a wholesaler? Of what? Is it a service business? What service?
- Why was the business started? What niche or gap in the market was being filled? What niche does it now target?
- What is the mission statement? What is the business philosophy? What are the driving principles?
- Who started the business? Who is involved in the business now? Who are the owners? Who are the managers?
- When was the business started? How long has it been around?
- How many employees does it have? What kind of people work for it?
- Where is it located? Where does it do business?

What Do We Do and Why Do We Do It?

This is the section in which you go into detail about your products and/or services. This is where the strengths of your business should be articulated. It is especially important to think about *why* you're offering these products and services. Here are some questions that can be addressed in this section:

- What does the business sell to its customers, specifically? If brand names are involved, which ones? Does the business have an exclusive in the marketplace? Is it a complete line? Or is it a specialty niche?
- Is the business a manufacturer? What does it manufacture? Does it involve high technology? Proprietary processes?
- Is the business a service business? What services does it perform?
- What is the price level: low, moderate, premium?
- What is the quality level: disposable, moderate, high?
- What are the strengths? What makes our business different from its competition?
- Why are we offering these products or services in the marketplace? Is it because we've always offered them? How have our products or services changed over the years? Or, is it because we've detected an unmet need in the marketplace?
- What specific niche(s) do our products or services fill?
- What image or position does our business have with its customers?

Who Do We Do It for and Why Do We Do It for Them?

This section should be a fairly detailed profile of your customers and potential customers. You should address the following questions:

- What is the marketplace, defined in geographic terms?
- Who are the customers? What do we know about them? How specifically can we describe them?
- Should we be finding out more about who our customers are? How can we find out more about them?
- Have our customers changed over the years? Are our customers going to change in the future? How?
- Do we have the names and addresses of our customers? If we don't, how can we get them? How are we storing them? How do we use those names and addresses? Should we be using them more?
- Who are our best potential customers? How much do we

know about them? Is there a way we can get their names and addresses?

- Why are our customers our customers? Why do they do business with us?
- Last, but not least, are there any holes in the marketplace? Are there any customer groups not being served that represent an opportunity for a new business or an expansion?

What Will Prevent Us From Doing It?

This is one of the most important sections of a marketing plan, and yet often the least well thought out. This is the section in which you articulate your weaknesses. This is where you give serious attention to your competition. This is where you look at other external factors that can prevent you from accomplishing your marketing goals. Some of the questions that should be addressed in this section include:

- What internal barriers or shortcomings does our business have?

- Is there sufficient day-to-day operating capital to buy stock, to promote, or to meet other bills? Is capital needed to expand a building or to update or buy new equipment?

- Do we need to build our inventory or reduce it?

- Do we need to add to our locations or close some locations?

- Do we have enough staff to get the job done, or do we need to reduce staff? Do I (the owner/manager) or my staff have the expertise and/or experience necessary? What areas do we need training in? Where could we get this training?

- Is the management structure appropriate for the job we're trying to do? Do the personalities of our people blend well?

- Who is our head-to-head competition, specifically? Who is our indirect competition?

- What are our competitors' specific strengths relative to us? Why do people do business with them instead of us? What, if anything, can we do to counteract their strengths?

• What are our competitors' weaknesses? What are we currently doing to exploit those weaknesses? What more could we do to exploit those weaknesses?

• What other external barriers could prevent us from reaching our marketing goals? Changing governmental requirements, such as environmental rules or safety regulations? Changing technology in our industry? Changing demographics of our customers? Other changes in our marketplace? Changing tastes of our customers or changing fashion? Difficulty in getting capital? Basic changes in our industry, such as mergers and consolidations? Changing requirements of our customers, such as higher quality or quicker turn-around time?

• Even if we can't always control these external forces, are there things we can do to mitigate their impact?

• Could some of these trends or changes represent an opportunity?

How Will We Promote Our Business?

This is the section in which you explore how you will let people know who you are, what you do, and, most important, how you will establish your uniqueness in the marketplace. In this section it's easy to get hung up on media and paid advertising. For some businesses, that may well be the bulk of the marketing program. But think broadly when you answer these questions, because for many businesses paid media advertising may not be the best promotional technique.

• Which major category of promotion will make up the bulk of our promotion (percentages are okay), paid media advertising, direct mail, personal sales, or some other category? Which category or categories of promotion will we use as our secondary approach, and to what degree?
• How will our promotion be different from last year's, and why?
• How will our promotion be different from our competitors', and why?
• Which specific media will we use, and how much will we use

them (percentages are okay)? Why are we using these specific media?
- Who is responsible for executing our promotions?
- Will we repeat our traditional promotions, such as an annual clearance sale or open house? Why?
- Will we have any new promotions? Are any special celebrations or promotions possible, such as a major anniversary?
- How can we use publicity as a promotional tool?
- Are there any opportunities for us in using telemarketing?
- Do we need to do a brochure about our business or update the brochure(s) we have?
- Are all of our front-line people sufficiently trained in our products and their benefits? Are they sufficiently trained in good customer service?
- Do we have a newsletter or other regular customer communication program? Do we have an easy way for our customers to talk to us, such as a suggestion box or survey card? Should we be doing more to communicate with and get information from our customers? If so, what?
- Are there any promotional activities we could use that don't cost much or anything? Are there opportunities for cooperative advertising with complementary businesses in our marketplace?

How Will We Know if We Have Succeeded?

This is the section where the rubber meets the road. This is where you've been headed in all the previous sections. This is the section for your marketing goals (your measures of success) and your action plans (how you're going to get there). By the way, since you can have as many action plans as you feel you and your business can handle, these pages do *not* count in my suggested length limits.

What Are Our Goals as a Business?

Here are some thoughts on developing goals:
First, most small businesses should have one or two major goals and perhaps another three or four secondary goals.
Second, these goals should be quantifiable and easily mea-

sured. For instance, they can be revenue goals, expressed as an overall annual dollar figure or as a percentage increase over last year. They can be profitability goals, expressed as a dollar figure or as a percentage of net profit. They can be sales goals, expressed as a dollar volume or as units. They can be growth goals, expressed as dollars or as units. Or they can be market share goals. For most small businesses, the major goal in the marketing plan will probably be a revenue or unit goal.

However, goals should be more than just dollars and cents or percentage increases in sales over last year. You can and should have specific goals for things like raising customer satisfaction levels, improving product quality, upgrading your staff through training or more qualified hires, increasing customer service levels, reducing service call response time, modernizing your equipment, expanding or redecorating your buildings, and holding promotions—whatever is important to your customers.

Revenue or sales unit goals can be easily measured, so monitoring your success level is also relatively easy. But what about some of those "touchy feely" goals like raising customer satisfaction levels or improving employee morale?

It is possible to measure changes in customer satisfaction or employee morale. You can conduct some kind of survey before you launch a program and then do a follow-up survey after you complete it to quantify any changes.

There are also indirect ways to measure your progress. You can monitor the level of customer complaints or product returns or employee grievances or whatever and see if these go down this year compared to last year. Or you can assume that implementation of the program will have some kind of positive effect, and simply monitor progress of the implementation itself. This is especially true of a program you might buy or acquire from somewhere else that has already established its effectiveness.

The point here is not that you will become a slave to some kind of complex monitoring system, where you must show progress on your goals or face a lashing with a wet noodle. Rather, the goal is to at least establish the habit of thinking in terms of progress toward your goals and to build in some periodic checkpoints that you can use to monitor that progress.

I'm not trying to send you on some kind of guilt trip if you don't achieve your goals. In fact, it's okay if you don't as long as you know why. That's the real value of a working marketing plan: to act as a road map of where you want to go. If you come upon some unexpected detour along the way and need to adjust your plan and/or your goals, so be it. But at least you know why you made the adjustment and you formulated a new goal to replace the old one.

What Are Our Action Plans?

Each of your goals should result in one or more action plans. Each action plan should include the following:

- A title for the plan.
- Which of the overall goals the action plan will help to accomplish.
- Specifically, what this action plan is supposed to accomplish—in other words, its individual goal.
- The specific steps needed to implement the action plan. The number of implementation steps is up to you. Some people prefer detailed to-do lists, and their action plans may have a dozen or more steps. Some are comfortable with less structure and might need only a half dozen or so major checkpoints.
- The time frame for implementing the steps and for the entire action plan. Again, the level of detail is whatever you're comfortable with. However, an action plan must have a time frame in order to monitor progress.
- Who is responsible for implementing the action plan.
- Resources needed to implement the plan—dollars, time, equipment, training, outside help.
- How you will know if the goal of the action plan has been reached. Specifically, what measuring stick will you use to decide success?

How long should an individual action plan be? Not more than two handwritten pages or one typewritten page.

How many action plans should you have? As many as your business and staff can handle. But that begs the question, so here is a rule of thumb that you can take for whatever it's worth:

- The minimum number of action plans you should have is one for each of the goals in your marketing plan.
- The average number of action plans you should have is roughly three per goal. This does not mean that you should have exactly three plans per goal; some goals require only one plan, whereas other goals might generate four or five.

Revenue and Expense Projections

This section of your marketing plan is not a full revenue and expense statement for your entire business. Rather, it includes whatever expenses and revenues are specifically relevant to your marketing plan.

For example, your business's overall expense budget might simply show a monthly line item called "marketing and advertising." This section gives the detail for that figure.

It shows the costs of your marketing programs spread over the year: media advertising, developing and printing of marketing brochures, direct mail campaigns, writing and mailing a customer newsletter, participation in shows or exhibits, an open house or some other special promotion, training for your staff, the expense for your sales staff.

Similarly, this section does not give your business's entire revenue projection for the year; rather, it shows the revenue you expect each individual promotion, such as a midyear clearance or a direct mail campaign, to generate.

Both expense and revenue projections should be broken down by month.

Attachments

This section includes any other documentation that you feel is important and/or relevant to your marketing plan, but that really doesn't fit into the main body of the plan. This might be copies of a survey form you intend to use. It might be the results of a customer demographic profile you've conducted. It might be a copy of a storyboard and/or script for a series of TV spots you're scheduling.

WHAT DO YOU DO WITH YOUR MARKETING PLAN?

You need to understand that a marketing plan for your business is not the same thing as a business plan, even though there is some overlap between the two.

Basically, a business plan focuses on the financial aspects of your business. It is a very detailed analysis of things like your costs and revenues, your market share, your growth potential, your cash flow, your accounts receivable and accounts payable, your tax position, your management experience and expertise, your management structure, your equity, your net worth as a business, your level of debt, and, perhaps most important, projections of your ability to repay debt (like a loan) or to generate dividends (for investors). While a business plan may ask for information on marketing, it has been my experience that this section usually ends up being cursory at best.

While your business plan is legitimately a confidential document meant for a limited number of eyes, your marketing plan, and by this I mean the answers to the six basic questions and your action plans, should be a highly visible document meant for as many eyes as possible within your organization.

Ideally, your entire staff (not just the owners or managers, not just the supervisors, but everyone in the place) should have a hand in writing your marketing plan and should get a copy of it.

The real secret of success for any marketing plan is not how brilliantly it's been put together. It's the extent to which the goals and action plans can become a daily presence in the operation of your business, a driving force behind everything you do. And the only way this will happen is if your front-line people buy into the plan, if they believe that it is their plan and that it will work.

Actually, the owner or manager can sit down all by himself and write a great marketing plan. But high-sounding goals that are only known to the owners or managers, and maybe to a few supervisors,

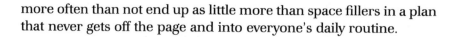

more often than not end up as little more than space fillers in a plan that never gets off the page and into everyone's daily routine.

Getting Started Tomorrow Morning

Have a marketing retreat.

Pick a Sunday afternoon or Saturday morning or a day when you are not open. Invite everyone on your staff to your home or to a meeting room away from your regular worksite. Tell them why they are being asked to come to this meeting. Strongly encourage them to attend, but make it clear that participation is voluntary.

Tell them to dress comfortably.

When everyone is gathered, you can go one of two ways:

1. You can have each individual actually write down an answer to each of the six questions that make up the marketing plan, then discuss the ideas as a group and try to come up with a consensus answer that everyone can agree to.
2. You can divide the group into six teams and have each team develop an answer to one of the questions. Then have each group present its answer to the whole staff, again with the goal of developing a consensus answer.

I would suggest that you spend approximately thirty minutes on each of the six questions, which means the meeting will be about three hours long. Feed them pizza and soda at the end!

If you get through all six basic questions and have reached a basic consensus on each, you've taken a giant step forward in developing a marketing plan and, even more important, in getting your people to have ownership in the implementation of the plan.

Almost certainly, a number of specific ideas for action plans will emerge from your discussions. Ask for volunteers, either individuals or teams, to take some of these ideas and develop them into action plans. If necessary, assign some people to write an action plan.

When the document is all done, the six questions are answered, and the action plans are written, make copies and share them with your staff. Yes, a cynic might suggest that one of your employees could take this plan and share it with your competitors, which would create all kinds of problems for you. But I would suggest to you that if you have an employee who is so unhappy that he or she would share your marketing plan with a competitor, you've got some serious internal problems that are worse than any external problem a competitor can cause for you.

A

A Glossary of Marketing Terms

Like all industries, marketing has developed its own jargon, including assigning some rather specialized meanings to otherwise everyday words.

action plan   The written steps of how a goal in a marketing plan or budget will be accomplished. It includes identifying who is responsible for accomplishing the steps, a time frame, and how success will be measured.

ad rate   How much a medium charges for paid advertising space or air time; also called *rate*.

advertising   Space in a newspaper, magazine, or newsletter and/or air time on a TV or radio station for which a sponsor pays a fee to have a particular message delivered.

advertising specialties   Items such as pens, coffee mugs, T-shirts and caps, key rings, and magnets that have been imprinted with an organization's logo and that are usually given away to customers and others for promotional purposes.

allowances   Reductions in price and/or rebates by manufacturers or suppliers to retailers to encourage advertising and promotion of their products.

audience   For the electronic and print media, a term used to designate their viewers, listeners, or readers; in advertising and public relations, the group the message is directed toward.

audience segmentation   The dividing of larger audiences into subgroups on the basis of specified criteria, such as similar demographic profiles, lifestyle characteristics, brand preferences, or media habits.

benefit   The specific positive personal gain that a customer perceives that he or she will receive from the use of a product or service or from an association with an organization. These are often the deciding factors in a buy decision.

brand loyalty/brand insistence   A very strong customer preference for a specific brand of product.

brand name   A unique and specific name for a product from a particular manufacturer. It is normally protected by being registered or copyrighted with a U.S. government office; see also *trademark*.

budget   A spending plan traditionally prepared on an annual basis. It includes goals to be achieved from the expenditures and a method for measuring and evaluating the results.

buyer   A synonym for *customer*; also the specific person responsible for buying supplies for a manufacturing company or products for resale.

buy decision   The point at which a customer makes the decision to purchase a particular product or service. The factors that lead to the buy decision are often complex and may be based as much on emotions as on rational considerations.

cold calls   Sales calls made on potential customers who have no previous knowledge of the organization and its products or services.

commercial   A television or radio advertising message; also called *spot*.

competition   A business or organization that offers essentially the same or similar products or services in approximately the same marketplace as you do. Almost all of today's marketplaces are highly competitive.

consumer show   An exhibit in which manufacturers and/or retailers in a more or less defined industry display their products or services to the general consumer. Examples are boat shows, camping and RV shows, and sporting goods shows.

coop (cooperative) advertising   An allowance or reimbursement offered to a local retailer by a supplier or manufacturer for advertising specific brand name products.

coupon   A promotion in which a discount is offered, usually on a specific product but sometimes across the board, as a means of encouraging trial of a new product or generating traffic. Coupons are generally distributed through print media (newspapers, magazines, shoppers) or by direct mail.

customer   In the traditional sense, any individual or organization that purchases products or services from you. In the broadest marketing context, any person or organization who receives your products or services, even if someone else pays for them—for example, clients of a human service agency.

customer letter   A promotional piece in a letter format addressed specifically to a business's current customers.

customer service   A fundamental marketing concept that says that a business's products or services, as well as its policies and practices, must all be centered around meeting the needs of its customers rather than its own convenience.

customer service representative   An inside salesperson who coordinates and facilitates the timely completion of a customer's order.

customer survey   A questionnaire or survey designed to solicit information and/or feelings from customers. Customer surveys are conducted to help a business evaluate how effectively it is meeting customer needs and to identify potential unmet needs that might lead to new business.

dealer brand   A brand of product that is sold exclusively by a specific store or chain, the opposite of a national brand; also called *private label*.

defensive marketing   A marketing strategy adopted by the market leader that is designed to protect the leader's dominant position. Only the market leader can adopt a defensive marketing strategy.

demographics   Specific economic, social, or lifestyle characteristics that may be used to describe a given audience group, such as gender, age, income, occupation, or household size.

direct mail   Using mailed marketing materials, such as brochures and catalogs, to promote a business or organization; also called *direct marketing*.

distribution   The transportation and storage steps through which a product passes in moving from the manufacturer to the customer. It is often complex and utilizes numerous intermediaries.

door-to-door selling   A sales technique in which sales representatives make cold calls on adjacent homeowners, going from door to door until they find someone interested in the product.

emotional appeal   Using emotions and feelings, rather than reason and logic, to sell products. The cosmetics, soft drinks, and fashion industries emphasize emotions in their promotions.

features   In marketing, the unique attributes of a product or service that differentiate it from its competitors. They are usually stressed in promotional materials and advertising.

focus group   In market research, a group of people who have been brought together to participate in a guided discussion about an organization, a product, or even a specific ad campaign. It is designed to gather qualitative information instead of quantitative data.

follow-up call   A second or subsequent call, after the first contact, by a sales representative on a potential customer.

Four Ps   A fundamental concept in marketing that says there are only four major areas in which a business can exercise control: the product it offers, the price it charges, the place at which the product is available, and how the product is promoted.

free-lance   A self-employed writer or artist who will do specific projects on a fee basis.

gatekeepers In industrial sales, receptionists, secretaries, or others who control the access to buy-decision makers, but have little or no involvement in the decision-making process.

goal A specifically defined objective in a marketing plan or budget. To be truly effective, it must be quantifiable and therefore measurable in some manner.

habit In marketing, a powerful and crucial force in many customers' buying patterns, such as "always" shopping for food at one particular store or "always" buying a certain brand of pain reliever. Getting customers to change long-established buying habits is a major promotional challenge.

hypercompetitive A term meant to emphasize that in many of today's marketplaces there are more competitors who are competing more aggressively than in the past.

image The specific positive feelings and attitudes you want to convey to your target audience through your marketing and promotional materials.

influentials Persons who are of particular importance to a business or organization. They can be key customers, trend setters, suppliers, community leaders, regulators, or political figures.

key customers The relatively few individuals that account for a majority of a company's business. In industrial sales they are often referred to as *key accounts*.

lifestyle A detailed profile used to help marketers and advertisers identify and define different customer groups. It generally includes information on attitudes, personal feelings, and preferred activities.

local media Newspapers, magazines, shoppers, television and radio stations, and cable systems that are based in and serve mainly a local market area; see also *national media*.

logo A distinctive type style and/or graphic symbol used to identify a specific organization, brand, or product name. It is normally protected by being registered with the appropriate U.S. government agency.

mailing list A list of names and addresses of people or businesses you wish to reach. It can be either a list that you gathered or one that you acquired from someone else.

mass marketing The marketing of goods or services to very large customer groups on a national or even global basis.

market The group a product or message is directed toward. Media talk about their market usually in geographic terms, sometimes in demographic terms; advertisers will refer to their customers and potential customers as their market group; similar to *audience*.

market profile A more or less detailed description of a market group using demographic, lifestyle, and geographic characteristics. It is usually developed through market research.

market research   The unbiased gathering of detailed information about a market group using methods like questionnaires, surveys, focus groups, and interviews to assist in making better marketing and/or advertising decisions.

market segmentation   Dividing a larger market group into smaller segments or categories that have similar demographic or lifestyle characteristics. For example, campers can be divided into backpackers, tent campers, and RV owners.

marketing   All the activities an organization engages in to facilitate the sale of its products or services in the marketplace. It is the most basic function of a business or organization.

marketing mix   The four basic marketing areas (product, price, place, and promotion) over which a business has control and their interdependence; see also *Four Ps*.

marketing plan   A detailed plan of how a product or service will be marketed.

marketplace   The arena in which a product or service is offered. It can be defined in geographic terms and/or in demographic or lifestyle terms.

message   The specific idea or feeling that an organization wants to get across to a target audience through advertising or other promotions.

mission statement   A brief statement designed to express an organization's basic purpose in as simple terms as possible.

multiple decision makers   In industrial sales, a term referring to the fact that a buy decision, especially for large-ticket items, often involves many different people at different levels of management.

national brand   A product brand that is sold through many different outlets and is advertised and promoted on a national or even global level; opposite of *dealer* or *private brand*.

national media   Television networks, radio networks, cable superstations and newspapers, magazines, and other publications designed to serve national audiences.

news release   Information in written form released to the media for use as news; also called *press release*.

newsletter   A publication issued periodically (usually biweekly, monthly, or quarterly) that is directed at the information needs of a very narrowly defined audience.

niche marketing   A term referring to the serving of a relatively small and specifically defined segment (niche) of a larger market by a usually small, specialized marketer; opposite of *mass marketing*.

offensive marketing   Aggressive marketing strategies adopted by startup

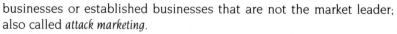

businesses or established businesses that are not the market leader; also called *attack marketing.*

opportunity   A specific need of a market group that is not currently being met or is being inadequately met and that, therefore, is available for a marketer; sometimes referred to as "a hole in the market."

order getter   In personal sales, a person who, through good sales techniques, patience, and persistence, can call on noncustomers and generate new orders for products or services.

order taker   In personal sales, a person who is good at serving existing accounts (taking orders), but is not effective at creating new business.

personal sales   A marketing effort that involves personal, one-on-one contact between customers and the business's sales representatives.

pinpoint marketing   A marketing effort directed at an extremely specific and tightly focused target audience. It implies even more precision than target or niche marketing.

place   One of the basic Four Ps, the aspect of marketing dealing with how the product makes its way from the manufacturer to the consumer. It includes decisions like what distribution channels will be used and locations of retail outlets.

point-of-purchase (POP) promotion   Posters, banners, special displays, or other types of promotions right in the store where products are purchased.

position   The image a particular business or organization is trying to establish, as in "He's positioned for the carriage trade."

potential customer   Someone who may buy your product. A basic tenet of marketing says that not everyone in a given marketplace is a potential customer. True potential customers are those people who more or less fit your customer profile, but who are not now customers.

price   Another of the marketing Four Ps, the aspect of marketing dealing with what price will be charged for a product or service. It involves decisions like how much markup is necessary to be profitable and whether a premium price will be charged.

product   The aspect of the marketing Four Ps involving decisions about the product itself, such as its design aspects (will it be utilitarian or decorative?) and its quality level (will it be "throwaway" or last a lifetime?).

product bulletin   A brochurelike promotional tool that usually focuses on the complete specifications and technical aspects of a specific model or product. It is generally used as a leave-behind piece or handed out at trade shows.

product life cycle   A concept that says that all products or services have a four-stage life cycle: introduction, adoption, maturity, and decline. For trendy products like hula hoops, the life cycle may be measured in weeks or months, whereas for durable products like the automobile, it may be measured in decades.

product segmentation   Offering multiple variations of a basic product in order to appeal to different target markets. For example, a snack cracker might offer its traditional cracker, plus a low-salt variety, a whole wheat variety, and a cheese-flavored variety.

promotion   Another of the marketing Four Ps, the aspect of marketing dealing with how a product will be promoted to the customer. It includes decisions like adopting a logo, package design, advertising, direct mail, and public relations.

public relations   As part of a business's promotion strategy, a broad spectrum of activities designed to present the organization in a positive manner, such as through news releases, speeches, and sponsoring special events.

publicity   The mentioning of a company, its products, or its employees in the editorial or news portions of a print or broadcast medium.

pulling   A manufacturer using direct consumer promotion, like media advertising and coupons, to create a demand for a product—to, in effect, "pull" it through the distribution and retail channels.

pushing   The opposite of pulling; a manufacturer using strategies like offering retailers a cooperative advertising allowance or paying incentives to store personnel for "pushing" a new product.

rational appeal   A sales appeal based primarily on logic. It generally focuses on a product's unique features and the benefits to the customer; the opposite of *emotional appeal*. This type of appeal is favored by most manufacturers and suppliers and by retailers of high-tech equipment.

reminder advertising   Media advertising that is intended to reinforce a business's ongoing identity and/or image; the opposite of *new product advertising*.

sales presentation   A personal contact with one or more customers or potential customers by a salesperson. It can run the gamut from an informal social call to a formal presentation with brochures and even audiovisual aids.

sales promotion   Nonadvertising techniques and materials, including contests and sweepstakes, point-of-purchase displays, special events, coupons, and brochures, designed to promote the sale of a product or service.

sampling   Giving away small quantities of a product either by direct mail or by handing them out at a store.

secret shopper   A person who shops the competition on a more or less regular basis to monitor prices, changes in products or services, and customer service.

special event   A tent sale, open house, anniversary celebration, trunk showing, radio remote broadcast, exhibit, or other event designed to generate traffic for a business.

spot   An ad on an electronic medium, such as a thirty-second spot.

Standard Industrial Classification (SIC)   A system of categorizing businesses. In marketing, it is especially useful to manufacturers and suppliers, who can identify their customers by their SIC code, then send direct mail marketing material to noncustomers in the same SIC code.

substitutes   Products or services that, while not directly competitive, for many people are an acceptable replacement. For example, a customer might really want barbecue-flavor potato chips, but notices that pretzels are on sale and accepts the substitute because of the favorable price differential.

target audience   The specific group you wish to reach with a promotional message. The more specifically defined this group is, the better.

target market   A somewhat broader term than target audience. It is usually used to define a geographic area or population group that is the focus of a marketing program.

team selling   A personal sales technique that is growing in popularity in high-tech industries. It involves a team of salespeople, usually consisting of a relatively nontechnical initial salesperson backed up by one or more technical experts who discuss the specific applications of a product or service.

telemarketing   Using telephone solicitation as the primary focus of making initial contacts with potential customers.

trademark   A name, word, and/or graphic element used to identify a specific brand name product or organization. It is legally protected by being registered with the appropriate U.S. government office.

trade publication   A periodical designed to meet the specific information needs of a particular industry or subgroup of an industry.

trade show   An exhibit in which manufacturers and/or suppliers display their products or services to buyers and/or owners and managers within a more or less specifically defined industry. Examples are hardware shows, home gift and decorative items shows, and new seasonal ready-to-wear fashion shows.

B

Three Sample Marketing Plans

SAMPLE MARKETING PLAN 1

This plan is for an established small manufacturer of custom high-precision measuring instruments.

Who Are We?

We are Acme Precision Instruments of Lake Geneva, Wisconsin. We manufacture and sell custom high-precision liquid and gas metering instruments for the food processing industry. We sell on a national basis. Our business was established in 1979 by two engineers who left a large instrument manufacturer to serve this specialty niche.

Our mission is to be responsive to our customers' needs and to deliver the highest-quality instruments on the market.

We currently employ thirteen people, including two administrative/clerical, two sales, three design/installation engineers, and six production/ shipping.

What Do We Do and Why Do We Do It?

Our specialty niche is the design, manufacture, and installation of custom high-precision gas and liquid metering instruments for food processing operations. We are not an off-the-shelf manufacturer. No two projects we do are exactly alike.

Our products are priced according to the project. Our prices are generally considered "high" compared to off-the-shelf instruments. However, we have many testimonials stating that the precision of our instruments allows significant savings on raw materials by eliminating waste, that our instruments have fewer repair and calibration problems requiring service, and that our instruments have a longer operating life than off-the-shelf instruments and, therefore, are cost competitive over time.

Although our instruments are extremely precise, they are analog-based; that is, they use mechanical measuring techniques and require manual adjustments.

We believe our strengths are:

- We have identified and are in the dominant market position in a specialty niche.
- We are responsive to our customers' needs.
- We have a nearly fifteen-year reputation for quality work.
- Our two principals are involved in the design/installation phase and are known throughout the industry.
- Of our thirteen staff members, four have been with us from the beginning and four more have been with us for at least five years—they believe in what we are trying to do.

Who Do We Do It for and Why Do We Do It for Them?

Our customers are food processing plants. According to the most recent U.S. Department of Commerce estimate, there are 16,658 operations in the SIC codes of our possible customers in the United States. These include dairy and cheese plants; wine and beer makers; processors of other liquid foods, such as juices; processors of dry food, such as cereal makers; and large food-product-related processors, such as corn syrup operations.

However, not all of these are potential customers, since in many cases off-the-shelf instruments will serve their needs. It is our estimate that between one-fifth (3,331) and one-fourth (4,165) of the possible customer universe will at some point need or want a precision instrument such as we make.

Since 1979, we have done 456 projects for 178 different customers; 46 of those 178 have had at least four projects and have accounted for not quite 58 percent of our total revenue. In the last four years, approximately 80 percent of our business has been from previous customers and 20 percent has been from new customers.

We have our own mailing list of 2,364 names in 949 different companies. These include all of our previous customers, plus names we have collected from personal sales calls, from trade show contacts, and by monitoring trade publications. There are commercial lists available that we can purchase to reach other potential customers.

We believe there is significant growth potential in our specialty niche:

- We have done projects for less than 5 percent of the existing potential market.
- As the industry moves more and more toward maintaining high quality and controlling costs, there will be a growing market for our precision instruments.
- There is a large new potential growth area involving the use of computer-based telemetry techniques to not only measure but automatically monitor and control gas and liquid flows.

What Could Prevent Us From Doing It?

There are two major problems that Acme Instruments faces.

The first problem is adequately serving the potential customer group based on our current design and technological capabilities. We believe that to do this, we need to:

- Add to our staff one design/installation engineer, two skilled production people, and one administrative/clerical person. The approximate annual cost is $160,000 to $170,000.
- Add at least 4,500 square feet, and preferably 6,000 square feet, to our manufacturing and warehouse/shipping area. The approximate additional cost is $25,000 to $30,000 annually for an existing building, plus the cost of moving, or $250,000 to $300,000 for new construction. We have space on our lot for an addition of this size.
- Add CNC (computer numeric-controlled) machining center. Specifications are to be developed; the approximate cost is $60,000 to $75,000.

The second problem is that in order for Acme to maintain its dominant position in the market group it serves, it will be necessary for us to offer our customers computer-assisted monitoring and automated control devices. One of our major goals for this coming year will be to develop a detailed plan and budget for entering this market.

An assessment of our competitive situation:

- There are four large, well-known manufacturers of off-the-shelf instruments (three overseas and one in the United States) that offer similar instruments to our customer group. Although it is possible that any one of these might enter the custom instrumentation market, none has shown any sign of doing so.

It is our best estimate that one or more of these will enter the computer-assisted automated metering and control product market, but there is no indication that any of them are doing so at this time.

• There is a custom instrument maker that serves the petroleum and chemical industry. We have had contacts with this company, and it has told us that it is not interested in getting into the food service industry, just as we are not interested in the petroleum/chemical industry.

A possibility might be for us to fund the research and development for computer-assisted monitoring and automated control systems jointly and license the technology to ourselves for use in our respective market niches.

How Will We Promote Our Business?

Up to now our promotion strategy has been to position ourselves so that when any customer needs a custom measuring instrument, we are the ones they call. We have done this through:

• Sending a direct mail packet once a year to a commercially purchased mailing list of businesses in the SIC codes that fit our customer profile, plus our own mailing list, a total of about 14,500 pieces.
• Having a booth at the national trade show for food processing manufacturers. We pass out informational brochures and do follow-up calls to any possible customers who give us a card or express interest.
• Responding to any phone and/or written inquiries with an initial phone call, then a personal call.

For the coming year, we will do the following:

• 1994 will be Acme's fifteenth anniversary. We will develop a brochure about the history and development of Acme and direct mail it to all our customers; we will also use it as a handout at trade shows and as a leave-behind piece for sales calls. We will engage a free-lance writer or public relations firm to do this project. Costs to be determined; we will budget up to $5,000.

• We will look into holding a by-invitation open house for our key customers, the forty-six who have done four or more projects with us. The open house would include a tour of our facility and a presentation by our principals and other staff, plus golf or other recreation time in our area. Cost to be determined; we will budget $60,000.

• We will also have the free-lance writer or PR agency (see above) put together a proposal to produce a video tour of our plant and some of our major projects. The video could be used at exhibits and for sales calls. Costs to be determined; we will budget $25,000.

How Will We Know if We Are Successful?

We have three major goals for the coming year:

1. The first goal is to develop a specific action plan and budget for conducting the research and development on computer-assisted monitoring and controls. The plan will include identifying sources of funding for the research, including exploring a joint venture with the complementing instrument firm.

2. The second major goal is to further strengthen our relationship with our key customers. We will accomplish this goal through the anniversary brochure and the open house.

3. Our third major goal is to develop a specific plan and budget for expansion, including identifying our specific space needs, designing a building, developing costs, and investigating sources of assistance (local or state economic development programs?).

SAMPLE MARKETING PLAN 2

This plan is for a soon-to-be-opened small retail business selling relaxation gadgets and tapes in a medium-size college town.

Who Are We?

The name of our business will be The Relaxation Shop. We will be located in a restored historic building in downtown Ithaca, New York. We will be a retail store, selling books, voice and music tapes and CDs, and gadgets that are designed to promote a more harmonious spirit (relaxation) and reduce stress.

The owners of the shop are a husband and wife team:

- Edward J. White, Ph.D., an associate professor of psychology at Cornell University. His studies have specialized in the prevention and reduction of work-related stress.
- Nanda (Verdi) White, a native of India. She is a qualified instructor in Yoga and T'ai Chi.

We believe the time is right to establish this business because:

- There has been an increasing enrollment in our workshops and classes on stress reduction and relaxation in the last two years, possibly indicating an unmet need.
- We have been reading in both the scientific journals and the popular media of a growing interest in people taking responsibility for their own well being.
- We are aware of similar shops that have opened with some success in other college communities over the last two years.

What Do We Do and Why Do We Do It?

We will sell at retail:

- Gadgets, games, puzzles, and sophisticated toys that are designed to promote relaxation and reduce stress. We expect this area to be approximately one-half or more of our business.
- Books, magazines, manuals, posters, greeting cards, art prints, and other printed materials. These will emphasize the area of personal and spiritual growth. We expect this to be one-fifth to one-fourth of our business.
- Cassette tapes and compact discs, both voice and music. These products will emphasize personal and spiritual growth and new age music. We expect this to be one-fifth to one-fourth of our business.

Most of these products are available from various other sources, mainly catalogs and, to some extent, retail outlets in larger cities, such as New York. A very limited selection of some of these products, mainly books and some tapes and CDs, are available at other local retail locations. There is no local outlet for gadgets, games, puzzles, and toys of the type we intend to stock. We believe there is a niche for the convenience of finding all these products in one hometown retail outlet.

Our products are not basic necessities, such as food, clothes, or medicine. Our products will be purchased as gifts, either as gifts for someone else or as gifts to oneself.

Who Do We Do It for and Why Do We Do It for Them?

Our customers will be characterized mainly by the following:

- Adults over thirty; this group will be 60 percent of our customers. The other 40 percent will be college-age students.

- About evenly divided between men and women.
- Mostly college educated or in college.
- Mostly in white-collar occupations, including professionals, business owners and managers, and educators.
- Mostly in the middle to upper-middle income bracket.

The common denominator among our customers will be an interest in personal and spiritual growth and/or holistic health issues.

They will be our customers because of the convenience of finding these products in one hometown location.

We expect that between 50 and 60 percent of our business will be local. However, within approximately one hour's drive are five other colleges, including two large state universities, and several larger urban areas. We think that the local market support will be sufficient to keep the doors open, but that the degree to which we are successful over the long haul will depend on how much business we can pull in from outside the local area.

What Could Prevent Us From Doing It?

We envision three possible major problem areas:

1. We may be misreading the level of interest in personal and spiritual growth and holistic health; in other words, the potential customer group may not be as large as we think.
2. The local market may not be large enough to generate sufficient business for us to even cover our expenses.
3. We may not be able to pull in business from outside of the area.

This could result in:

- At worst, exhausting our working capital so that we have to close
- At best, only a marginally profitable business

Other possible problems include:

- A major change in the national and or local economy (recession) that would affect people's attitudes about buying nonnecessities
- One or more of the other local retailers that now offers a limited selection of these types of products expanding its offering to be a more direct competitor

How Will We Promote Our Business?

Promotion will be a major challenge for us. We think we know pretty well who our target group is; the difficulty is in finding the media and other promotional methods to reach them on a cost-effective basis.

For our grand opening we will concentrate mainly on the local market. We will do the following:

- Run a 3 by 5 ad four to six times in the local daily newspaper and at least twice in the college newspaper.
- Run thirty spots (fifteen each during the seven days of our grand opening) on the two commercial FM radio stations that have high listenership among adults. In addition, we will make a contribution to the college FM station that will qualify us for a weekly mention as a supporter of the station.
- Hand-address postcard invitations for our grand opening to the college faculty, the medical community, and friends.
- Send a packet of news releases about the shop and the owners to all local media and to media within a roughly sixty-mile radius, hoping to generate a feature article or two.

After the grand opening, the major thrust of our promotion for the local market will be:

- To secure as many guest appearances as possible on the electronic media (TV and talk radio) to talk about relaxation and stress reduction. We will focus on the "gee-whiz" gadgets and toys as visual aids. We will phone producers of TV public service shows and radio talk shows and send them our news release packet and cover letter explaining our idea. We will follow up with phone calls.

- To make as many appearances as possible before community groups, business luncheon groups, and others who have programs. Although the talk will focus on relaxation and stress reduction, we will demonstrate the gadgets and toys as visual aids. We will pass out copies of our brochure to all who attend these programs.

- To send a bimonthly newsletter to our own mailing list. The list will include customers (people who visited the store during the grand opening), selected professionals and business leaders (we'll get their names by watching the newspaper and other sources), and friends. The newsletter will feature announcements of new products and workshops and tips and advice on relaxation and stress reduction.

• To schedule lectures and workshops, and possibly even a periodic weekend retreat, featuring experts on relaxation and stress reduction. These will be promoted through the newsletter, news releases to the media, and possibly an ad in the local paper.

The major thrust of our promotion outside of the area will be news releases to the media within a roughly sixty-mile radius announcing our workshops and lectures.

How Will We Know if We Are Successful?

Our goals are to:

• Generate a total of $36,000 in gross revenue for the first twelve months, or be averaging $3,200 per month in revenue ($800 per week) for the last four months of the year.
• Generate at least 350 names on our mailing list by the end of the first six months and at least 500 names by the end of twelve months.
• Generate at least six positive mentions in the media (new business announcement, feature story) during our grand opening and at least six more (with at least three of these being in out-of-town media) during the remainder of the first year.

SAMPLE MARKETING PLAN 3

This plan is for a new program being created by an established human service agency in a rural county of northern California.

Who Are We?

We are Family Support Services of Lassen County, California. We are a human service agency that has provided adoption and family and youth counseling services to the area since 1938. Our main office is in Susanville, which is in the southern part of the county. We also have an outreach office in Madeline, in the northern part of the county.

Our mission statement: It is the mission of Family Support Services of Lassen County to strengthen and assist families in crisis and to keep families together to the greatest degree possible by providing a comprehensive array of positive, family-oriented support services.

This is a marketing plan for our new Be-a-Friend Project, which will recruit, train, and place volunteer befrienders for shut-in and/or otherwise restricted activity elderly persons.

Lassen County is located in the northeastern section of California. It is a large county, measuring over 100 miles across diagonally. Much of the county is mountainous and is characterized by undeveloped national forest. There are many small communities, isolated settlements, and back-country farms and ranches.

What Do We Do and Why Do We Do It?

As more and more of our young people leave the area for larger cities for their education and/or jobs, and as our older citizens are living longer, we are finding an increasing number of elderly people living alone throughout the county.

Most of these elderly are healthy and independent and are more than able to take care of their everyday needs. However, many are not, because of:

- Increasing frailty as a result of advancing years
- Inability to drive, either because they never learned how or because they have lost the ability
- Loss of a supportive spouse
- Failing health

What are we finding is that while many of these elderly people are in need of some form of assistance, they do not need or want someone to do things "for" them, such as social workers or homemaker aides. Rather, what they want is a small degree of help in taking care of themselves; that is, they want to maintain the dignity of self-reliance and independence as long as possible.

The Be-a-Friend Project will recruit and train people to provide that small degree of assistance. The kinds of activities a Be-a-Friend volunteer might be involved with are to:

- Telephone the elderly person several times a week just to say hi and see how he or she is doing.
- Visit him or her once or twice a week.
- Take the elderly person to the store or on errands.
- Take him or her to a movie, lunch, or some other social activity.
- Perhaps invite the elderly person to his or her home on holidays.

The Be-a-Friend Project will have four major components:

1. Participant outreach, which will consist of a worker who will recruit the elderly participants
2. Volunteer recruiting, which will consist of a worker who will recruit volunteer befrienders
3. Training of volunteers, which will be shared by the two workers, plus other Family Support Service staff and outside guest lecturers
4. Placement and follow-up, which will consist of a worker who will match volunteers with participants, place volunteers, do follow-up visits, and handle any problems that might arise

Who Do We Do It for and Why Do We Do It for Them?

As we see it, we have two distinct target groups:

1. The elderly participants. The outreach worker will identify possible participants through referrals from community service agencies, elderly service agencies, health service agencies and clinics, churches, and friends. We expect that the majority of participants will be females over age seventy. They will be geographically scattered throughout the county, with many in rural and/or isolated areas.

Although one of the goals of the outreach worker will be to develop a more accurate estimate of the number of potential participants in the county, it is our best guess at this time that it is between 200 and 300. We have consulted with other community or human service agencies in the planning of Be-a-Friend, and there is general agreement with this estimate.

2. The volunteer befrienders. The recruitment specialist will secure volunteers through media appeals and presentations to interested community groups. Although there will be no restrictions on the age or gender of the volunteer friends, we expect that there will probably be half again as many female volunteers as male and that the majority will be over forty-five but under sixty-five.

The project has received a three-year demonstration grant from the California State Commission on Aging, so funding is not an immediate problem. However, based on past experience with grants from various sources, the project will need to be cognizant that potential long-term funding sources will constitute a third target group beginning in the second year and will be a major priority during the third year.

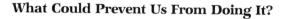

What Could Prevent Us From Doing It?

The possible barriers to a successful Be-a-Friend Project include:

- Lack of interest on the part of participants and/or lack of sufficient numbers of participants; that is, not enough in-need elderly are found or those that are found do not wish to participate.
- Lack of sufficient numbers of interested volunteer befrienders.
- Geographic or transportation problems, for example, difficulties in matching volunteers with participants in isolated parts of the country.

How Will We Promote Our Project?

It is the consensus of the planning group that aggressive and continuous promotion of the Be-a-Friend Project will be the key to its success. This is particularly true of the recruiting program for volunteers. The first-year promotion program will include:

- Creating the Be-a-Friend logo to provide continuing identity for the project. The logo will consist of a bumblebee with the word *friend* engraved on it. It will be used on brochures, in slide presentations, in public service ads, and as a pin that volunteers will wear.

- Developing an initial brochure about the project. It will outline the goals of the project, its purposes, and who can participate. It will stress how to become a volunteer and what it means to volunteer. It will feature Family Support Service's involvement. The brochure will be handed out at all presentations.

- Developing a slide show about the project for use with presentations.

- Developing a quarterly newsletter for volunteers. The newsletter will include program updates, provide ongoing volunteer training through advice articles, and feature brief volunteer profiles. Besides being mailed to volunteers, the newsletter will also be mailed to community leaders and handed out at group presentations.

- Doing presentations to virtually any group that will listen: community groups, church groups, business groups, professional groups. We will actively solicit opportunities to do presentations to the groups by sending them a letter asking if we can be on their program calendar and making follow-up calls if necessary. The outreach worker and the recruiting specialist will be jointly responsible for setting up and conducting the presentations.

- Seeking major support from the local media. We will consult with the daily and weekly newspapers that circulate in our area to develop a feature article about the project. We will contact the producers of news and public service shows at television and radio stations in our area. And we will contact the community affairs directors of the television and radio stations to secure regular public service ads and contact the newspapers to try to arrange regular house ads on behalf of the project.

How Will We Know if We Are Successful?

Our first-year goals are to:

- Develop a brochure and slide show about the project.
- Develop a quarterly volunteers' newsletter.
- Make no fewer than twenty-four presentations about the project to groups (or an average of two per month).
- Secure no fewer than four major media mentions of the project (such as a feature article in the paper or a guest appearance on a news or public service show) and no fewer than eight other media mentions (such as a public service announcement on the radio or a house ad in the newspaper).
- Recruit no fewer than thirty-six participants and thirty-six volunteer friends (or an average of three per month).

C

The American Marketing Association

If you are interested in more information about marketing, I recommend that you look into joining the Chicago-based American Marketing Association. The Association publishes a wonderful tabloidlike newspaper called *Marketing News* that is just packed with ideas, tips, and information on marketing trends. The group also sponsors seminars and workshops on various areas of marketing. You can contact it at

> American Marketing Association
> 250 S. Wacker Drive, Suite 200
> Chicago, IL 60606–5819
> (312) 648–0536

Index